The Philippine–American War (1899–1902)

A Captivating Guide to the Philippine Insurrection That Started When the United States of America Claimed Possession of the Philippines after the Spanish–American War

Free Bonus from Captivating History (Available for a Limited time)

Hi History Lovers!

Now you have a chance to join our exclusive history list so you can get your first history ebook for free as well as discounts and a potential to get more history books for free! Simply visit the link below to join.

Captivatinghistory.com/ebook

Also, make sure to follow us on Facebook, Twitter and Youtube by searching for Captivating History.

Contents

Introduction

The Philippine-American War of 1899–1902 was a dramatic, world-changing conflict that shaped the century to come and revealed the early stirrings of America's drive for global power. The conflict and its aftershocks continue to influence the Philippines and the wider region to this day, leaving a legacy of governance, society, and economic organization. The Philippines today is an important American ally and a counterbalance to the growing Chinese power in South Asia, but the history between the United States and the Philippines has not always been as friendly as some may imagine—in fact, American-Filipino history is soaked in blood and defined by brutal, devastating combat. The Philippine-American War is, perhaps, something that many Americans and Filipinos would like to forget about, particularly in light of Filipino-American cooperation against the Japanese invasion of the Philippines in the Second World War, but it's vital to study and understand the Philippine-American War in order to see a clear picture of what led to the world we know today and comprehend the scale of imperialism and military conquest that has defined the past centuries.

The Philippines is a group of around 7,600 islands speaking 89 different dialects that sits more than 8,000 miles away from the continental United States. The islands span more than 1,200 miles from north to south. The population of the Philippines was estimated to be around 8 million in the late 1890s, while the United States population at that time was around 76 million. Running the Philippines from Washington, D.C., was a tall order indeed, and the decision to try to do so would erupt into a prolonged and bloody war.

In terms of the historical background, the Philippine-American War emerged out of the lessening strength of the Spanish Empire and the desire of the United States government and related economic interests to establish a strong foothold in Asia. Power players in the American government and business community were very interested in snatching up slices of Spain's global empire before other countries could do so. Spain had successfully colonized many nations in South America and around the world but was widely viewed as incompetent and exploitative when it came to their administration of colonial Cuba and other nations.

In terms of the Asian sphere, Spain had ruled over the Philippines since the 1560s, profiting from its fertile soils and exploiting its native inhabitants ruthlessly. Native Filipinos—*Indios*—had staged ongoing attempts to be free of colonial rule and determine their own future for over 300 years. Insurrections in the Philippines started with Filipino Catholic priests who were tired of the Spanish church leadership telling them everything they had to do and say, and tensions were sparked particularly in 1872 with the execution of three Filipino rebel priests. Finally—and temporarily—they succeeded in 1898, one year after General Emilio Aguinaldo had become the leader of the rebelling Filipinos and six years after Aguinaldo's fellow revolutionary, Andrés Bonifacio, had founded the revolutionary Katipunan society. Often referred to as the "Father of the Philippine Revolution," Bonifacio was instrumental in the Filipino effort for independence from Spain prior to the Philippine-American War.

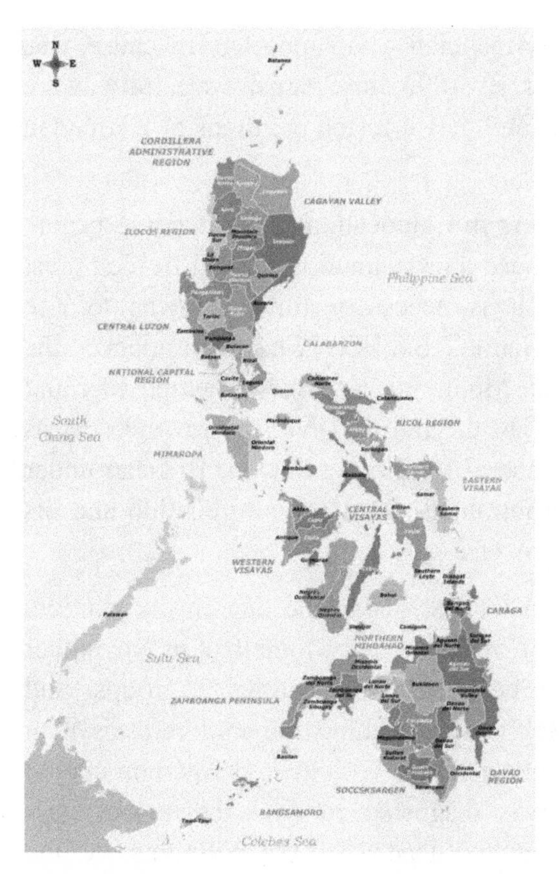

Map of the Philippines. Image Credit: Public Domain

After founding Katipunan and advocating armed revolution, Bonifacio and his compatriots expanded their reach from Manila to other regions, including Cavite, Laguna, Bulacan, Pampanga, Batangas, and Nueva Ecija. Bonifacio became the "Supreme President" of the Katipunan society in 1895 and worked with local councils to coordinate resistance to the Spanish. They wrote newspapers and patriotic materials to rally the people, and the influence began spreading into Luzon and Panay. By 1896, the membership of Katipunan is estimated to have been around 40,000.

Aguinaldo was a member of the Katipunan society who was hesitant about the need to start armed resistance and wanted to get more firepower and outside backing first. General Antonio Luna, widely known as a brilliant military tactician who supported the cause, was brought on board to help out. By 1896, the Spanish were fully aware of how far things had gone, and they arrested hundreds of Katipunan members.

Bonifacio rallied the members in Caloocan, and the uprising began. By August 28, Bonifacio issued a proclamation that all fit men must join their army, saying, "it is necessary for all towns to rise simultaneously and attack Manila." Sneakily, Bonifacio attacked the nearby town of San Juan del Monte instead, seizing gunpowder and supplies from the Spanish. By the fall of 1896, the revolution was focused in Cavite under General Emilio Aguinaldo, Bulacan under Mariano Llanera, and Morong under Bonifacio. Aguinaldo and his men took control of Cavite by October.

Bonifacio continued to be a vital leader in the ongoing revolution, which included the taking of Marikina and Montalban in November 1896. Tensions broke out between rival Katipunan groups, and Aguinaldo did not like Bonifacio, claiming the middle-class man was arrogant and behaved like a "king" who looked down on others. Bonifacio, for his part, was disgusted to find that upper-class Aguinaldo was regarded as the leader of the Filipinos by the Spanish, not him.

Aguinaldo commanded that Bonifacio be arrested in April of 1897. Aguinaldo said he had received a letter that accused Bonifacio of burning a town and its church since the town wouldn't supply his soldiers. There were also complaints that his forces stole water buffalos from the villagers. Aguinaldo's emissaries went to Bonifacio's military encampment under friendly pretenses and then attacked his camp the next day. Bonifacio was stunned and commanded his men not to fire on fellow Filipinos. He was shot in the arm and stabbed in the neck. Bonifacio's wife was raped according to some reports, and his brother Ciriaco was killed. Bonifacio was tied up in a hammock half dead and brought to Aguinaldo.

Bonifacio—as well as Procopio, Bonifacio's other brother who survived the attack—were tried for "treason" with no ability to mount a defense and the prosecution comprised entirely of Aguinaldo's men. Bonifacio and his dead brother were found guilty and sentenced to death, and they were executed on May 10, 1897. The execution is highly controversial to this day, and Bonifacio is seen by some as the actual first President of the Philippine Republic, not Aguinaldo who would later declare himself as being such. Moreover, certain close friends and colleagues of Bonifacio, such as Emilio Jacinto and Macario Sakay, never recognized Aguinaldo as their leader, which would lead to very important events later on during the war with the Americans.

Despite his early death, Bonifacio's leadership and organizational abilities had put the cause of Filipino independence ahead by decades, and by 1898, the Filipinos were about to finally get rid of Spain. This was precisely when the United States entered a short, successful war with Spain. Officially due to Spain's attack on the USS *Maine* at Havana Harbor, the Spanish-American War was prompted by sympathetic portraits of the abused Cubans who had been under Spanish rule for centuries. The American media highlighted Spanish atrocities against the poor natives and stirred up American desire to liberate Cuba from the Spanish—and gain a vital sphere of influence in their own backyard. The Spanish were widely portrayed and seen as backward. They were lazy, evil, and Catholic; the Americans, on the other hand, were hardworking, enlightened, and Protestant. It was the American mission to liberate the world from the duplicitous slovenly Spaniards at any cost necessary.

As part of the Spanish-American War, the United States added the Philippines as a strategic target for good measure, sending equipment and aid to Aguinaldo and his men and eventually entering the fray. For America, the Philippines was a second front against Spain to tie up their naval power and troops and prevent them from deploying to oppose American assaults on its possessions in Cuba. For the Filipinos, it was a chance to push Spain out for good.

The Filipino nationalists and militia fighters wanted independence and freedom. Although the idea of the Philippines as a united "nation" in the Western sense was still fairly new, they defined themselves in contrast to their European colonizers. The American government had very different plans: they wanted to teach the Philippines self-government and how to run efficiently as an economy and society—by taking it over and controlling it. Seventy thousand US troops later and three horrific years of fighting with hundreds of thousands of starved and diseased civilians would make an 1898 *New York Times* editorial that said American rule would help the natives "learn the duties of freedmen" seem quaint and deluded in retrospect.

America started the 19th century with the First Barbary War in Tripoli and ended it with a fight against the First Philippine Republic in the Philippine-American War. The 20th century, of course, would prove to be even more tragic and conflicted. Historian Bernard Fall has called the Philippine-American War America's "First Vietnam," while historian James Hamilton-Paterson has called it the "least-known war" in American history. It's certainly true that readers and students will hear much more about the brief and much less deadly Spanish-American War than they will about the Philippine-American War. And yet the conflict is very important, both geopolitically and historically, for a myriad of compelling reasons.

From the American side, the background of the Philippine-American War was all about the drive for economic and military might combined with American religious fervor and the nationalistic belief in "Manifest Destiny," which was considered to be God's will for the United States to expand and gain global power. Despite this being a widely shared analysis retrospectively, in reality, the conflict was more of something that the United States stumbled into, due to a combination of perceived necessity, patronizing and racist beliefs about foreign non-white people, and economic and military interests, rather than marched into.

The Philippine-American War is not generally a focus of the American educational curriculum, nor is it often featured in Western popular culture, for two main reasons. For one thing, the world wars of the 20th century and the horrors of the Vietnam War eclipsed this conflict that occurred so long ago; for another thing, the Philippine-American War is not a proud chapter in American history because it exposes a raw push for power and dominance from the US government and a leadership fueled by rampant racism, greed, and arrogance. Internment camps, starvation, torture, intentional targeting of civilians, and civilian food storage by American forces: these are the shameful legacies of the Philippine-American War. Heroes were made and killed, monsters rose out of the battlefield, and, sadly, the innocent suffered most of all, grimly foretelling the diabolical bloodshed that would be inflicted on civilians in the world wars of the 20th century.

Any reader who wants to understand the modern world, particularly in Southeast Asia, will be fascinated, appalled, and shocked to read the chaotic, surprising, and tragic accounts of what happened as American forces battled the First Philippine Republic from 1899 to 1902. Despite the end of declared hostilities by 1902, sporadic combat continued until 1913. The exact number of dead and wounded soldiers is unknown but ranges between 4,234 to 6,165 American servicemen killed with an estimated 2,818 wounded and approximately 34,000 Filipino fighters killed with the numbers of the wounded unknown. Devastatingly, an estimated 200,000 to one million Filipino civilians—depending on which source one consults—perished as a result of the conflict, the majority from starvation and disease that was, at the very least, encouraged and abetted by US forces as a tactic of war.

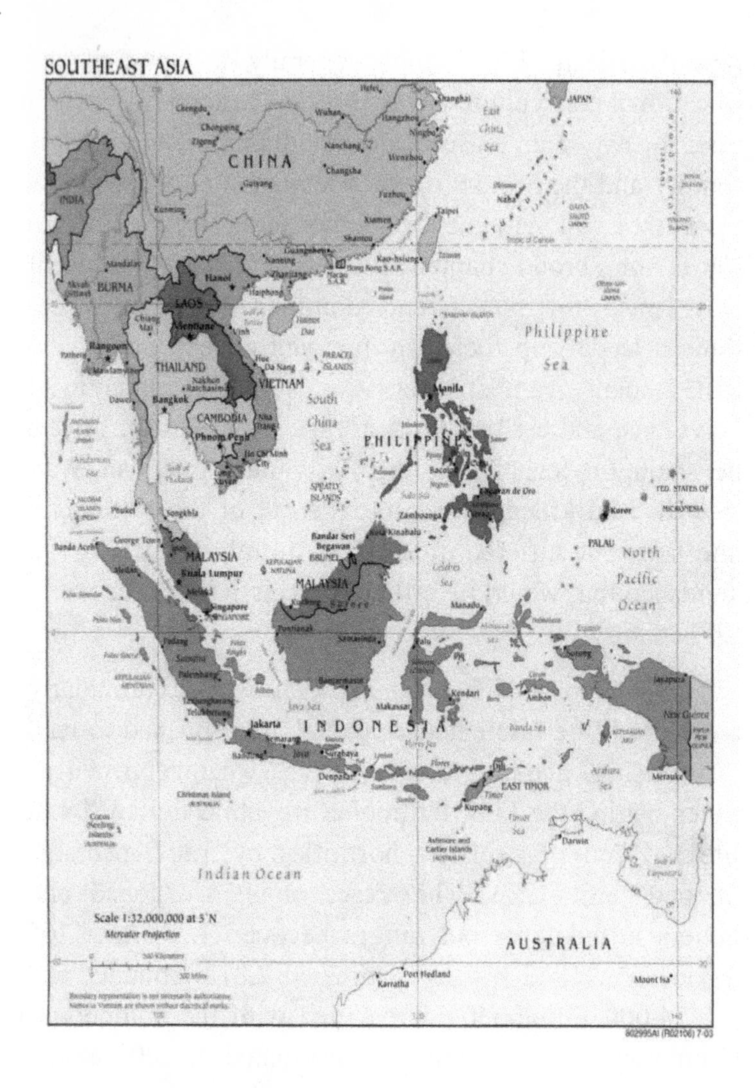

Map of Southeast Asia. Image Credit: Public Domain

The Philippine-American War was far bloodier than the Spanish-American War but often receives less attention in the educational system and media. It is, however, a highly prophetic and disturbing conflict, foreshadowing the wars to come in the 20th century and exposing the rift in late 19th century America about foreign interventionism, national interest, and military strategy. The Philippine-American War was the real starting point of America's decision to deploy sustained troop presences and naval power to the Asian sphere and dedicate time and energy to open up the Asian economic market; almost a century later, American President Richard Nixon would famously travel to China in the 1970s to discuss and open up trade. From the Filipino perspective, which is very important for Western readers to consider and understand, the war had a profound effect and continues to shape the Filipino society, government, and worldview up to the present day, including class and race perceptions, the understanding of their national identity, structures of local governments, and the relationship with the modern United States, as well as conceptions and expressions of contemporary patriotism.

Chapter 1 – Manifest Destiny vs. Self-Determination

The United States, at the time of the Philippine-American War, was fully awash in an ideology that emphasized its own importance and responsibility to bring civilization and Protestantism to the rest of the benighted and ignorant world. Completely shirking the concepts of European colonialism and imperialism, figures like President William McKinley saw America's role as essentially establishing order in an unstable world because it was the right thing to do. In an interview about the Philippine-American War, President William McKinley characterized the acquisition of the islands as a divine gift that was America's destiny to accept and make the best of, despite some misgivings. Although he understood the risks and criticisms of such a move, McKinley presented the situation that placed the Philippines into American hands as something that was simply too opportune to be mere chance and was clearly a mission from on high.

> When I realized the Philippines had dropped into our laps I confess I did not know what to do with them...And one night late it came to me this way—I don't know how it was, but it came: (1) That we could not give them back to Spain-that would be cowardly and dishonorable; (2) That we could turn

> them over to France and Germany-our commercial rivals in the Orient—that would be bad business and discreditable; (3) That we could not leave them to themselves—they were unfit for self-government—and they would soon have anarchy and misrule over there worse than Spain's was; and (4) That there was nothing left for us to do but to take them all, and to educate the Filipinos, and uplift and civilize and Christianize them, and by God's grace do the very best we could do by them.

The concept of Manifest Destiny was a powerful one in 19th century America. It helped propel the westward pioneers in the 1840s into the Great Basin (an area that spans nearly all of Nevada), California, the Pacific Northwest (commonly seen as including the states of Oregon, Washington, and Idaho), Utah, and Texas and continued at a quick pace following the horror of the US Civil War. Settlers firmly believed that it was America's destiny to expand and gain territory, and so did American leaders. In 1867, the United States purchased Alaska from Russia for just over seven million dollars, and in 1878, the US government signed a treaty to get a naval station in Samoa. Twenty years later, in 1898, they annexed the island of Hawaii, and that same year, the short war with Spain launched America as a dominant imperial power with global standing. One year later, Secretary of State John Hay issued a proclamation that the United States had equal trading rights with China like any other European power, including Great Britain, who had formerly colonized and economically opened China to the West. America was also fixated on the idea of China's "open gates" and the prospect of invigorated Asian trade as well as gaining numerous coaling stations to refuel its naval forces; the Philippines would soon provide both.

More broadly, the United States, led by President McKinley, was entranced by the idea of shaping the Philippines to their economic and ideological liking. They were ready to do whatever was necessary to increase America's world standing and power. In this case, they considered that what was necessary was to make the

Philippines completely under their control. The problem was that other than Manila, the rest of the islands were still run by Filipinos backed by freedom fighters who hoped America would recognize their desire for independence but who were ready to fight hard if that turned out not to be the case.

Underlying many of the debates and conflicts of this time were also the ideas and convictions of social Darwinism, which essentially argued that struggle, conflict, and the pursuit of domination were inherently healthy, necessary, and inevitable and would lead to a fitter, healthier, and more productive humanity. The fittest would survive as nations as people fought to the death, but in the end, it would be best for everyone that the weak, sick, unintelligent, and the superstitious "savages" be weeded out of the gene pool and replaced with superior Anglo-Saxon civilizations to lead a better, richer future. These ideas were often used in support of imperialism, racism, and eugenics.

The arguments of imperialism and colonialism won the day in the United States as they entered the war with Filipino nationalists, but as the awfulness of the Philippine-American War dragged on, some parts of the American public became horrified and turned against it politically and socially, particularly by certain anti-imperialist factions in the United States government headed by politicians like 1900 presidential candidate William Jennings Bryan (most famous for his "Cross of Gold" speech). More broadly, however, most members of the American public simply did not care and did not register the war on their radar, only occasionally glancing at biased news coverage that told them about the horrific, backward Filipino natives and their merciless killing of Americans for no reason. Ultimately, the horrors of the conflict contributed to decades of foreign policy restraint in the United States out of concern that their next engagement could go down a similar path as the war in the Philippines.

From the Filipino side, the Philippine-American War was all about the fight for independence and national self-determination. It was also about inter-Filipino racial divisions, economic class divisions, religion, and geography. The Philippine-American War was also far more complex than two unified, singular nations going up against each other in the heat of battle. Similar to other archipelagos, the Philippines was inhabited by a wide range of indigenous peoples and different ethnic migrants from various surrounding areas, like the Malays who had migrated, intermarried, fought, and settled various islands in a wide territory inhabited by many historically linked and interrelated peoples.

The Spanish had first broken ground on the Philippines when Ferdinand Magellan landed at Cebu in 1521. The Spanish took a strong interest in the resource-rich island chain and its potential to grant them more military and economic prowess for the crown and the pope. Spanish explorer Ruy López de Villalobos named the island chain *Las Islas Filipinas* in 1543, in honor of Prince Philip, who would go on to become King Philip II of Spain, as well as the king of Portugal. Hemp, tobacco, coffee, and geopolitically crucial areas to project Spanish military might were siren songs to the power-hungry Spanish Empire, which was convinced of its own racial, religious, and governmental superiority, perhaps to an even greater extent—and more blatantly—than the Americans who were to come during the Philippine-American War.

A Spanish settlement was built on Cebu by 1565 under the leadership of Manuel López de Legazpi, heralding three centuries to follow of dominant Spanish rule. Catholicism had been enforced by the tip of a sword or imprisonment on the Filipino islanders, who populated around 1,000 of the Philippines' 7,600 islands. Many converted to Catholicism, and intermarriage became common, creating a considerable middle-upper class of partly Spanish ethnic citizens as well as the fully Spanish upper classes. The city of Manila became the focal point of trade and Spanish military power for the duration of the Spanish colonization. Other than some Muslims in the southern island area, most Filipinos converted to Catholicism or at least kept their own native religions to themselves and practiced outward worship and obedience to Spain's Catholic demands. Trade with China and Mexico ran through the Philippines and filled the Spanish coffers with riches as they sailed galleons full of silver, spice, silk, and porcelain to their different markets. The Spanish established a feudal economy built on exploiting the poor natives and rewarding the richer mixed-race Filipinos and pure Spanish upper-class elites with more opportunities and power.

The three main racial divisions in Filipino society at the time of the Philippine-American War had the *Peninsulares* at the top: white Spanish Filipinos born in Spain who had immigrated to the Philippines. *Peninsulares* tended to be the richest and regarded themselves as vastly superior, more intelligent, and entitled to respect and obedience. In the middle were the *Insulares*, who were individuals of Spanish descent born in the Philippines and who were plentiful in the merchant and political class. At the bottom were the *Indios*, or native Filipinos, who filled the ranks of the working class and were treated more or less as worthless garbage by most of the other members of society, with many remaining illiterate. Many of the *Peninsulares* and *Insulares* sided with the Americans quite early on in the war, seeing it as more in their interest to ally with a rich foreign power as long as their own economic dominance was not jeopardized.

Somewhat ironically, the opposition to Spanish rule began among Filipino priests, who resented the direct Spanish domination and the control of the Roman Catholic Church on the islands. In the late 19th century, Filipino intellectuals and the middle class began calling for independence. Sporadic uprisings of the *Indios* through the centuries had always been ruthlessly squashed by the Spanish *Peninsulares* and *Insulares*. The rebellions were not well organized or armed well. By the late 19th century, however, an organized Filipino resistance began to spring up, including an 1872 rebellion in Cavite and, eventually, the 1896 Filipino Revolution which rallied under the banner of the Katipunan society (the *Kagalang-galangang KATIPUNAN ng mga Anak ng Bayan* or, in English, the Supreme and Venerable Association of the Children of the Nation). An estimated 20,000 Filipinos rose up against the Spanish, propelling 27-year-old Emilio Aguinaldo into the spotlight. He became the head of the Katipunan by 1897, rallying the troops with an idealistic nod of homage to American and European ideals of liberty and brotherhood. "We deserve freedom and honor too," Aguinaldo told his followers. "Filipino citizens! Let us follow the example of European and American nations. Let us march under the Flag of Liberty, Equality, and Fraternity!"

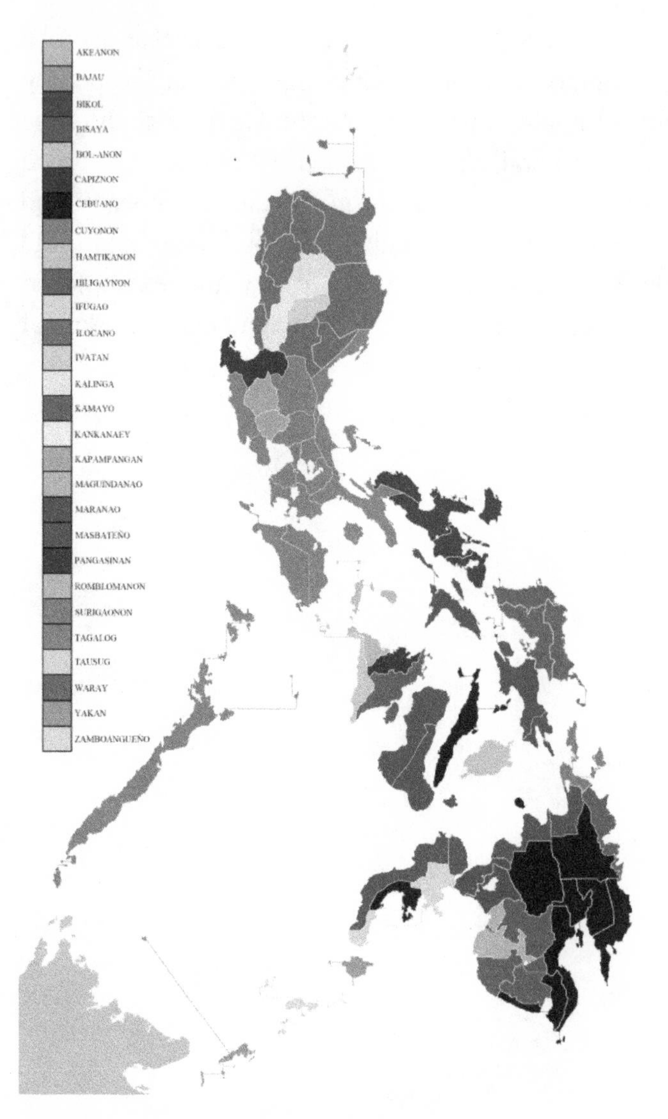

Map of the Philippines showing ethnic groups. Image Credit: Public Domain.

The Filipinos were comprised of a number of tribes, ethnicities, and religions, across the islands, often unconnected by any sense of unified "nationalism" or integrated patriotism in the European sense. Although national identity had been strengthened and forged somewhat during the centuries of Spanish rule, it was still very much secondary in an overall sense. Being Tagalog, Moro, Malay, or any other tribal group was much more important than being "Filipino," particularly considering that independence leader Aguinaldo's Tagalog ethnic group was intensely disliked by a lot of the other tribes who had been historically dominated by them. Tribes such as the Igorot, Apayao, Cebu, Palawan, Moros, and Negritos had inhabited the numerous islands of the Philippines for centuries, and a lot of their histories included conflict and complex interrelations with the Tagalog majority. For them, Aguinaldo still represented the dominance of the Tagalog, and as such, the Americans sought to exploit this existing tension, building up the Filipino upper classes and supporting those groups who felt marginalized and threatened by Aguinaldo and the Tagalogs.

Chapter 2 – The Waning Power of Spain

After defeating the Spanish possession of Mexico by 1848 and gaining more territory including Texas, New Mexico, and California, the United States was chomping at the bit to wrest more land and resources away from the Spaniards. It was the American ticket to world power, after all. The American government wanted to project American power around the globe, and they were willing to use whatever force necessary to do so. Part of this was due to the high-minded beliefs about the superiority of American ideals, part of it was due to the social Darwinist glorification of war, and part of it was the simple lust for military and economic power.

The prevailing view was that Spain had not done a good job in the Philippines and had not left it very industrialized or efficient, and the Americans wanted to cripple Spain's ability to use the Philippines for resupply or naval support. American author Trumbull White bemoaned the Spanish administration of the Philippines and expressed a common American outlook about the incompetence and corruption of Spain when he wrote that "the natural resources of the Philippines are very good, and under a civilized administration, these islands would be rich and prosperous. But the mildew of Spanish misgovernment is upon everything."

By the end of the 19th century, the Americans had their chance to take another piece of Spain's colonies by seizing the Philippines. Not only did they feel morally justified in doing so because of supposedly "liberating" the poor Filipinos from the powerful Spanish kingdom, but helping take the Philippines would put a stake through the heart of Spain's Asian sphere of influence and give America valuable coaling stations for their navy, strategic ports, and an economic outpost in the heart of the Asian trade routes. Spain had controlled the Philippines for almost 400 years, but the United States had plans to change that.

The primary cause of the Philippine-American War was the brief and dramatic war that took place between the United States and Spain in 1898. This was preceded by Aguinaldo's and his men's ongoing uprising against the Spanish which, although successfully held at arm's length from seizing power, had exhausted and frustrated the already strained Spanish Empire.

The background to this was the ongoing revolt that Aguinaldo and his fighters had been carrying out against Spain. The Spanish nation had already had to deal with constant uprisings on an almost yearly basis, and it was beginning to get worn down by the constant combat. As the late 1890s approached and Aguinaldo and his fighters continued to encroach on Manila, Spain came up with a temporary solution. Spain had too many troops committed to Cuba and other colonies to finish putting down an all-out uprising in the Philippines, so it offered Aguinaldo a truce if he would move the Katipunan's headquarters to Hong Kong and pull back his fighters. They also paid the already wealthy Aguinaldo an undisclosed amount of money to do so and agreed to limited reforms related to land ownership, several very modest changes in favor of political rights for Filipinos, and a few minor economic benefits. Although he did not trust the Spanish, Aguinaldo needed the money for food and weapons. Although his family was wealthy and he hailed from the upper class, Aguinaldo needed financial and logistical support to get his army fed and armed. He agreed with the Spanish to their terms in order to gain the much-needed supplies, although he was certainly not surprised when the Spanish did not follow through on their various promises.

Meanwhile, as Aguinaldo languished in Hong Kong, America was heading for a major confrontation with Spain.

The 1898 Spanish-American War broke out after the February 1898 explosion of the American USS *Maine* in Havana Harbor. This incident occurred while colonial Spain was in the middle of brutally suppressing an uprising against the Spanish military in Cuba. Following the detonation of the *Maine*, the American media, namely the *New York Journal* and the *New York World*, owned respectively by William Randolph Hearst and Joseph Pulitzer, shouted for blood. The government and news media placed the blame squarely on Spain for attacking the United States in cold blood. Later historical investigations and analyses have shown that the explosion may well not have been done by Spain and may have been what is termed a "false flag" done in order to provide a *casus belli* or justification for war. In any case, the American public was outraged by the attack and by Spain's barbaric practices and actions against the Cubans in colonial Cuba. Although they saw the native Cubans as racially inferior, the principles of American statehood and individual rights stirred up feelings of indignation among the public against the cruelty and indifference of Spain.

On April 21, 1898, the Spanish-American War broke out and ended on August 13, not even lasting four months in total. Many historians agree that the Spanish-American War is what truly launched the United States as a world power. The Spanish-American War was brief and mainly fought on the water through naval battles, including an American naval intervention in Manila Bay and an American land force to route Spain's control of the Filipino capital.

Prior to the outbreak of the Spanish-American War, President McKinley's assistant secretary of the navy and future US president, Theodore Roosevelt, seized the opportunity to set up a preemptive knockout punch against Spain. Roosevelt was very much a man of action, who believed war and conflict were natural, manly pursuits and part of the survival of the fittest. As a college friend put it, Roosevelt "wants to be killing something all the time" and "would like above all things to go to war with someone." Writing to a friend about the Spanish-American War, in which he had fought as a volunteer, Roosevelt extolled its glory, remarking that it was "a great thing" and that American should feel immensely proud of doing its part and having had "luck to get into the fighting!"

Roosevelt had an idea for how to decimate Spain in the Asian theater of war and tie them down there as soon as war was officially declared between the US and Spain. Roosevelt ordered US Navy Commodore George Dewey to take the American fleet stationed in Hong Kong and sail to Manila in order to sink the Spanish fleet when war was declared with Spain. Roosevelt hoped to prevent Spain from deploying troops and ships out of the Philippines and using them to attempt to go help their compatriots in Cuba against the United States. Secretary of the Navy John Long, who had been away from work due to illness, returned to his office on February 25, and he said, "In my short absence I find that Roosevelt has come very near to causing more of an explosion than the *Maine.*" However, importantly, Long never canceled the telegrammed military order from Roosevelt to Dewey, perhaps on President McKinley's internal orders, although this is not made clear from the historical record. Roosevelt's decision turned out to be very effective, and paired with President McKinley's April 22 blockade on Cuba, it was a tightening vice grip on the Spanish Empire before the official outbreak of the Spanish-American War.

Under Roosevelt's standing orders, Dewey commanded nine ships from his Asiatic fleet in Hong Kong for the Philippines as soon as the war broke out between Spain and the United States. It's worth noting that Aguinaldo was on one the American ships, being returned from his exile in Hong Kong. Aguinaldo and Dewey had various clandestine meetings aboard Dewey's ship *Olympia*;

Aguinaldo also met with Captain E.P. Wood of the *Petrel*, who gave Aguinaldo advice, ammunition, and arms. He told Aguinaldo that once the Spanish were gone, he would not have to worry because America, being "great and rich," had no need or wish for colonies. It was simply a matter of preventing Spain from keeping its unearned power, not a matter of America gaining power, Wood assured him.

The whole mission was a big gamble, considering Dewey only had use of two supply ships and it was monsoon season with heavy torrential rains, making visibility and conditions difficult for naval combat.

After hunting for the Spanish fleet in Subic Bay and finding nothing except what Dewey remarked would be a great place for a naval base in the future, Dewey's fleet set out for Manila Bay and, upon finding the Spanish there, blasted the Spanish ships to pieces on May 1, 1898, in the area around the Filipino city of Cavite.

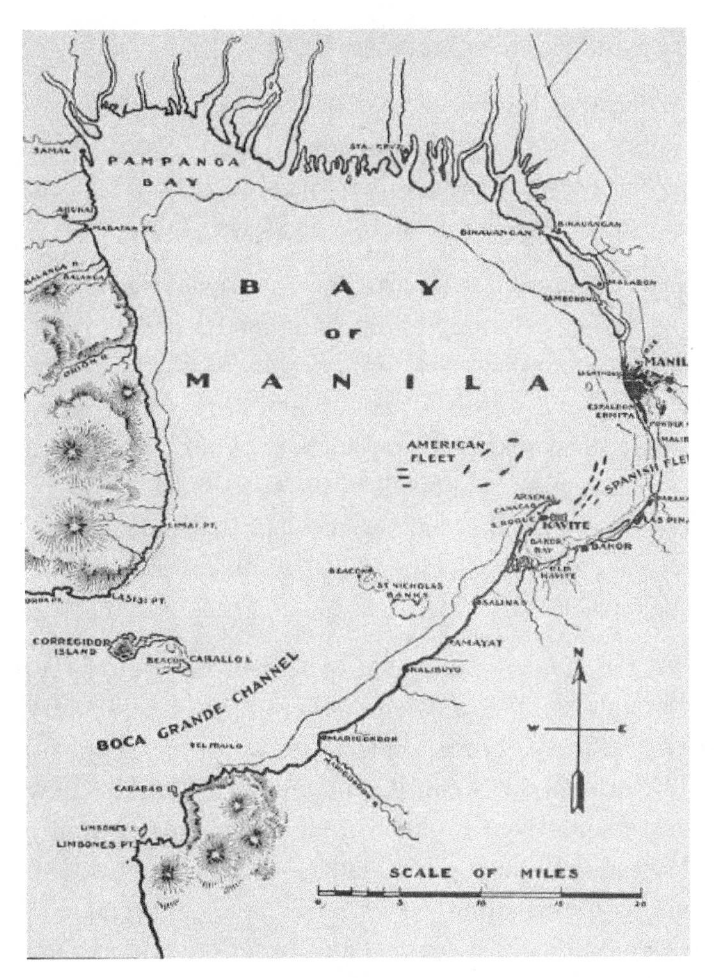

Map of Manila Bay, 1898. Image Credit: Public Domain

Spanish Rear Admiral Patricio Montojo's fleet was devastated, with three warships completely sunk, seven burned to a crisp, and hundreds of Spanish casualties. Montojo appears to have expected the disaster as he had already placed his outdated, weak ships in shallow waters so that more of his crew would survive the attacks and not drown in deep water after being racked by superior American firepower and naval technology. One American sailor was killed in action, and there were several very minor injuries on the American side, but overall, the mission was deemed a major success.

An observer to the battle described it thus:

> The shores around Cavite glowed bright with the flames of burning ships. Two of the Spanish ships looked like skeletons. The fires consuming them made their bones appear black against the white-hot heat, like a gateway to Hades.

Dewey was celebrated as an epic hero in American media and popular culture, with his face popping up on cigarette cases, mugs, and various patriotic paraphernalia. He became known as the epitome of bold action and a true American hero who had slapped the face of the arrogant Spanish and send them packing. Dewey was also promoted to rear admiral as a result of his success in the battle. Filipino nationalists were ebullient at the result of the naval battle, hopeful that America would now let them declare independence after years of combat against Spain.

Although he was not naïve, Aguinaldo had gradually begun to believe that American military power could act as a temporary safeguard against Germany, France, and Britain, whose powerful navies were lurking around the South Pacific and threatened his new independence movement. Even if the United States was not fully trustworthy, at least he had their word that they were committed to the same outcome as him: getting rid of Spain. Indeed, Aguinaldo noted down in his journal that Dewey had also promised him to back the Filipino Revolution and independence, promising "my word is stronger than the most strongly written statement there is." Unsurprisingly, Wood and Dewey would later deny both of their statements to Aguinaldo, saying they had promised no such thing.

Aguinaldo's soldiers, now led again by him since he had returned from Hong Kong (after a stint hiding in Singapore), along with Dewey, assailed the Spanish defenses for almost two months and had managed to blockade their access to water and food. Aguinaldo demanded Spain's surrender, but they were embarrassed to do so, also thinking they would be murdered once they did so. Not giving up, Aguinaldo spent time at his family's luxurious estate in Cavite, to the south of Manila, planning how to defeat Spain for the final time. The Spanish troops were in a highly defendable position inside Manila's enclosed Intramuros district, but Aguinaldo had troops from the American military coming to back him up and the power of their fleet behind his men. Even if his troops were outgunned, Aguinaldo felt optimistic because he had one of the most powerful countries in the world at his side, ready to lay down fire and help him get his country back. America was the ace up his sleeve, and Aguinaldo was ecstatic, writing,

> Divine Providence is about to place independence within our reach. The Americans have extended their protecting mantle to our beloved country, now that they have severed relations with Spain, owing to the tyranny that nation is exercising in Cuba. The American fleet will prevent any reinforcements coming from Spain. There, where you see the American flag flying, assemble in numbers; they are our redeemers.

Chapter 3 – An Uneasy Alliance

America now controlled Manila Bay, Aguinaldo and the nationalists controlled the islands, and Spain controlled the city of Manila. This tripartite arrangement was certainly not bound to last—and it would not last for long. Only two months had passed since Dewey had decimated the Spanish fleet in Manila Bay before America began sending troops to strengthen their foothold, supposedly helping the Philippines on its path to self-determination. An incoming force of around 11,000 American soldiers under Major General Wesley Merritt arrived on June 22, 1898, from San Francisco. A hardened fighter, Merritt had fought in the US Civil War, the American Indian Wars, and the Spanish-American War prior to combat in the Philippines. He was fully on board with the mission and not interested at all in the wider implications of the Filipino struggle for independence or the merits and drawbacks of an American empire. Merritt's soldiers were energized and ready for action, firing on Guam along their way to the Philippines just for sport. Guam couldn't return fire because it had no working cannons, and the Spanish governor hilariously emerged down to the shore with a white flag to explain why he hadn't returned fire. The bewildered Americans captured the governor right away, of course, eventually leading to the negotiation of a deal to establish Guam as a US possession.

After arriving in the Philippines, the Americans were granted a piece of land south of Manila by Aguinaldo as part of the siege against the Spanish. This was to be a team effort, considering that while the Americans had better equipment and guns, the Filipinos had the superior knowledge of the lay of the land, the fighting capability of the Spanish, and inside tips and strategies in how to inflict damage and retake the city of Manila. However, after Merritt arrived with his troops, he planned the American assault on Manila with Dewey without coordinating with Aguinaldo, making it clear that the Filipinos would be left out of the process. The Americans wanted to keep Aguinaldo far away from power or any real stake in the outcome because as soon as they landed, he became an impediment to the American project. Far from getting what he saw as his rightful place in taking back his country, Aguinaldo was marginalized away from the battle lines around Manila, with Dewey ordering incoming soldiers to take position on the outskirts of the city and replace Aguinaldo's fighters. Aguinaldo's "redeemers" had turned out to be less interested in redemption and more interested in replacing him and his men.

To be sure, Filipino fighters were America's *de facto* allies against Spain, but they were shocked and infuriated to find that the American troops pushed them out of positions surrounding the city. US troops herded them at gunpoint and explained that they were under orders to lead the assault on Manila. The Americans would not let the Filipinos assist in taking the city back from the Spanish or discuss what was to come next once Spain fell. This American policy established with complete certitude that the United States forces were there to call the shots—and shoot them as well—and that the Filipino nationalists were unwelcome to have anything other than a nominal role. After years of fighting for their independence, it was a humiliating and enraging turn of events.

Aguinaldo was already outraged by the Americans pushing his fighters out of the way in retaking Manila. His rage turned into a flat-out commitment to fight the Americans after the US forces engaged in backhanded dealings with the Spanish to hand over Manila to them. Spain had effectively already lost the war but was not comfortable or agreeable with handing it over to the Filipinos, who they saw as non-white savage opportunists and ignorant barbarians. Spain's governor, General Fermín Jáudenes, agreed with General Elwell Otis, a war veteran of the US Civil War and American Indian Wars, to a surrender of Manila if the Americans kept the Filipinos out of the new government. The Spanish, more content to surrender to a "civilized" and white European power, held a mock final battle with few casualties and gave Manila over to the American conquerors.

Manila "fell" on August 13, 1898, after around half a day of fighting, and American forces rapidly established control in place of the Spanish. Merritt was appointed by President McKinley as the first military governor of the Philippines. According to historian Dr. David Silbey, this fight was somewhat staged and was done by the Spanish garrison more so to "uphold their honor" than to actually attempt victory. The Spanish formally surrendered the city and began the months-long process of returning back to Spain. The Americans made sure to keep the Filipinos away from the victory parade and any militarily important locations, and Merritt organized troops to maintain tight control of the city. Merritt was relieved as the military governor to go take part in treaty negotiations with Spain, and General Elwell Otis succeeded him on August 30 as the next military governor.

The United States had promised to help and protect any Filipinos who assisted them against Spain. This was spelled out in a January 4, 1899, proclamation from Otis:

> In the war against Spain the United States forces came here to destroy the power of that nation, and to give the blessings of peace and individual freedom to the Philippine people, that

> we are here as friends of the Filipinos, to protect them in their homes, their employments, their individual and religious liberty; that all persons who either by active aid or honest endeavor cooperate with the government of the United States to give effect to these beneficent purposes, will receive the reward of its support and protection.

The reality was that once the Americans firmly held Manila—and later annexed the Philippines—any resistance would be put down by force, and those Filipinos who had helped the United States against Spain were now a problem, not an asset. US forces made it crystal clear that Filipinos who resisted American rule would be crushed by force if necessary. From the American perspective, Aguinaldo and his fighters were a thorn in their side, fighting for no good reason and irrationally resisting American leadership. In a cable to Secretary of the Navy John Long in 1898 prior to the war, Rear Admiral Dewey had precisely expressed this outlook, writing that "Merritt's most difficult problem will be how to deal with insurgents under Aguinaldo, who has become aggressive and even threatening toward our army."

In fact, as noted, Filipino soldiers had been hopeful that their help in defeating the Spanish would be rewarded by the Americans, who they expected would respect their ambitions of nationhood. America had been their hopeful *de facto* allies in ridding the islands of Spanish rule, but the reality was that America did not see the Filipino nationalists the way they saw themselves. The Filipinos saw themselves as revolutionary fighters, like America's citizens who rose up to fight for independence from Great Britain in 1776. Unfortunately for these Filipino nationalists, their hopes were soon dashed. The American government did not see them as heroic revolutionaries, seeing them instead as troublesome, racially inferior savages who needed to be crushed if they would not surrender to "civilized" American rule.

Meanwhile, Aguinaldo and his interim government met at a monastery north of Manila and planned an entirely different future, with Aguinaldo writing that "the people struggle for their independence, absolutely convinced that the time has come when they can and should govern themselves." Despite the drama of the summer and being excluded from the capture of Manila, Aguinaldo and his men moved ahead with forming their own government and declared independence from Spain in June of 1898.

They organized elections and created the Malolos Congress by September, which passed the declaration of independence and formally established the First Philippine Republic. The republic's constitution, which was the first ever established in Asia, separated church from state, granted civil rights, and allowed landowning males to vote—a norm for that era. Aguinaldo still controlled almost all of the Philippines except Manila and hoped that the United States would eventually agree to hand over formal control to his new government.

It was not to be.

President McKinley made up his mind to negotiate with Spain in Paris and see what came of it. American leadership, including McKinley, wanted to do a better job in the Philippines than the Spanish had and gain the valuable farmlands there and place the trade routes of the Philippines under American command. The Philippines just needed a strong hand and Anglo-Saxon superiority in order to optimize the economic and social situation, bring the natives to Christianity, and basically build a successful, democratic country along American lines.

Negotiations began on October 1, 1898, between Spain and the United States, eventually leading to various decisions.

At the signing of the Treaty of Paris between the United States and Spain on December 10, 1898, Cuba became independent if they agreed to American involvement in its governance, and Puerto Rico and Guam were transferred over to America without a peep. Aguinaldo was not present at the Treaty of Paris signing—nor were any Cubans or Filipinos whatsoever—as the opinions of the "natives" were not valued. It's worth noting, however, that Major General Merritt was present to aid in the deliberations.

Along with Manila, America had landed a deathblow to Spain's possessions in the Caribbean, Pacific, and Asia in terms of the Philippines and Cuba. It was a devastating turn of events for the formerly dominant Spain, and the treaty negotiations reflected Spain's significantly weakened position. It had holdings, to be sure, but it no longer had an effective military or naval power to back them up and was somewhat backed into a corner in terms of its leverage.

At the treaty, President McKinley addressed the importance of Manila as the spot for a Western Pacific naval base and decided that the Philippines must be run by the United States as they were not yet ready for self-government. The debate over accepting the Philippines as a US holding then moved forward to the US Senate.

The most important issue that came out of the December treaty was the decision to "buy" the Philippines from Spain. The United States acquired the Philippines under the treaty terms in return for twenty million dollars as payment for Spain's infrastructure investment which had been poured into the Philippines up until that point. This was infrastructure that, of course, had been largely constructed and designed in order to facilitate Spain's continual extraction of raw materials and wealth from the Philippines for its own benefit.

In his proclamation on December 21, 1898, "Benevolent Assimilation"—which the US Congress never oversaw or approved—President McKinley announced military governance across the Philippines and claimed that the Americans came "as friends to protect the natives" and bring "the mild sway of justice." Nonetheless, as the proclamation made sure to spell out, any acts of disobedience or sabotage by the Filipinos would be put down right away by "the strong arm of authority."

Now, America could use the Philippines for its own benefit, including as a laboratory to try out its benevolent ideals of democracy and economic liberalization—by opening the market and culture to American involvement and control. There was a fairly big problem, however. The Filipinos who controlled the islands of the nation besides the capital of Manila, which rested firmly in the hands of the Americans, had never agreed to be run by America.

During January 1899, an uneasy peace prevailed between Aguinaldo's forces and the Americans. Venereal disease rates among the US troops went sky high as bored servicemen frequented local prostitutes and dropped any morals they may have had back home. They were at war, after all. A British journalist at the time wrote that American soldiers frequently called the Filipinos "niggers," but real hostility or combat had yet to break out. They also started calling the Filipino people "gugu," a word which would later reemerge in a modified form during the Vietnam War as the common racial epithet used by American soldiers for the Vietnamese, "gook."

The Philippine-American War would finally arrive in early February of that year, leading to a bloody three-and-a-half-year conflict and hundreds of thousands of dead.

There were a number of additional causes of the war in addition to the struggle with Spain to seize its overseas assets. Firstly, the geopolitical ambitions of the United States to have a center of military power in Asia was in contrast to the Filipino fight for independence. Secondly, the Americans desired and the rich resources offered by the Philippines, including valuable raw materials such as rice, tobacco, and coffee, as well as the opportunity to economically expand and trade easier with China and other nations. Thirdly, the Americans believed in Manifest Destiny and desired to Christianize the Filipinos, who were widely viewed by the American elite as ethnically and religiously inferior.

The economic rationale was quite significant. With the geographical position of the Philippines and its historical importance as a route to China, the Americans coveted the kind of access to markets that could be granted for the boom of surplus goods that were being produced in the United States. They needed buyers and markets and a place to ship those goods from—not to mention all the additional goods and trade that could be derived directly from the soil and the factories and labor of the Philippines itself once American businesses and joint ventures moved in and put down a stake. As American Congressman Albert Beveridge put it:

> Our largest trade henceforth must be with Asia. The Pacific is our ocean. More and more, Europe will manufacture the most it needs, secure from its colonies and the most it consumes. Where shall we turn for consumer of our surplus? Geography answers the question. China is our natural customer...the Philippines gives us a base at the door of all the East...No land in America surpasses infertility the plains and valleys of Luzon.

Further American speculation on the economic value of the Philippines from Frank A. Vanderlip, an American banker and journalist, wrote about how important the archipelago was as a center for economic expansion into Asia, including Indochina and Indonesia.

> It is as a base for commercial operations that the islands seem to possess the greatest importance. They occupy a favored location, not with reference to one part of any particular country of the Orient, but to all part...Together with the islands of the Japanese Empire, the Philippines are the pickets of the Pacific, standing guard at the entrances to trade with the millions of China and Korea, French Indo-China, the Malay Peninsula, and the Islands of Indonesia to the South.

Another uncomfortable reason for the Philippine-American War was blatant ethnocentrism and religious bigotry. Significant portions of the American press and politicians viewed the Filipinos as worthless savages who needed the firm hand and leadership of white Americans. The darker skin tone of some Filipinos, especially the *Indios*, led to frequent comparisons of them to Native Americans and the frequent portrayal of them as "backwards," "unenlightened," or inherently evil in some vague, racist way. In their mind, the Filipinos needed to be ruled by white Americans for their own good, even if *they* didn't know it or accept it yet. The American elite and politicians, largely populated by Protestants, viewed the Filipino people as racially inferior because of their darker skin tone and Asian ethnicity, as well as their technological lack of advancement and their Catholicism and folk religions. February 1899—the year and month the war broke out—was also the year that Rudyard Kipling's poem "White Man's Burden" was published in the *London Times*, including its insistence that white Westerners must subdue "sullen peoples, half-devil and half-child," and goes on to exhort whites to colonize other people for their own good: "take up the White Man's burden/ Send forth the best ye breed/ Go bind your sons to exile/ To serve your captives' need."

A combination of condescending and paternal prejudice, as well as outright bigotry, prevailed among American decision-makers and eventually a vote to annex the Philippines and make it an American colony passed the US Congress—albeit by one vote.

It is important to note that the Philippines was never fully annexed as an American state or as a legal part of the United States per se, since this would have been scandalous at the time to include millions of non-white people—many of whom did not speak English and wanted to have their own country—into the white, "civilized" United States. Instead, it maintained a kind of quasi-status as a US possession under American governmental authority until it was granted independence by the US after the Second World War in 1946.

The fact that American leadership and intelligentsia largely viewed Filipinos as inferior is well illustrated in the following passage from

American journalist John Bass in *Harper's Weekly* on October 15, 1898, where Bass wrote that

> The Filipino is the true child of the East. His moral fiber is as the web of the pineapple gauze of which the women make their dresses. He will cheat, steal, and lie beyond the orthodox limit of the Anglo-Saxon. His unreliability and the persistence with which he disobeys orders are irritating beyond description; besides this, his small stature and color invite abuse.

If the passage strikes the reader as racially prejudiced and almost bizarrely hateful, that is because it is both.

The war to come would bear out this strong racial prejudice with the widespread murder of civilians, reminiscent of the later world wars of the 20th century and the conflicts in Vietnam, Korea, and Cambodia. While dehumanization of the enemy in conflict is nothing new and continues to this day in most countries and with most conflicts, it's very important to understand this attitude that prevailed among American leaders and soldiers in order to grasp the way that the Filipinos were viewed and the effect this had on making the conflict seem justified in American eyes.

A popular marching song for the US military expressed this outlook well:

Damn, damn the Filipinos!

Cut-throat Khadiac ladrones*[1]!

Underneath the starry flag

Civilize them with a krag**[2]

And return us to our beloved home!

---

1 *Thieves

2 **Rifle

Chapter 4 – Filipinos Prepare for Independence or War

When America defeated Spain in the Spanish-American War in 1898 and capped it off by coming in to claim the victory in the Philippines, it was simply the finish to a war that had essentially already been won by Aguinaldo and the Filipinos.

Despite America's insistence that it was now in charge, Aguinaldo signed the Philippine Declaration of Independence on June 12, 1898, two months before the Spanish were defeated by the Americans at Manila. He set up a representative government with a separation between church and state and the recognition of various rights for citizens. He was moving ahead with independence in the face of the American incursion, causing considerable unrest. As far as the Americans were concerned, Aguinaldo had played his part through years of fighting to wear Spain down and let them come in for the big win. Now was his time to step aside and let Uncle Sam run things. The reason that the United States cared about Aguinaldo and his nationalists was that Aguinaldo and his men already held most of the Philippine territory, including the key Philippine island of Luzon, when the Americans arrived. Manila alone would not give the United States real control or usage of the Philippines as an Asian outpost.

By all accounts, the Filipinos were governing themselves with reasonable competence, having appointed a Cabinet and written a constitution. The Americans were not interested in this experiment in self-government despite all the idealistic American rhetoric about democracy back in the states.

The Filipinos simply wanted their own country and had just finished fighting the Spanish in a drawn-out insurgency during the Philippine Revolution (also known as the Tagalog War) from 1896 to the falling of Manila in the summer of 1898 after centuries of uprisings against Spanish domination. They were violently rebelling against 333 years of Spanish colonialism and won a hard-fought victory.

As mentioned, instead of granting Filipinos their independence after their grueling victory against Spain, the United States arrived, ready to take up where the Spanish had left off. America swooped into the power vacuum with guns blazing, holding Manila and formally annexing the Philippines in the US Congress. This turn of events was devastating to the Filipinos, who were still very angry about being pushed out of the victory over Spain at the last moment and sidelined into bit players by the Americans.

In his "Call to Arms," Filipino leader Emilio Aguinaldo explained that he had outlined his reasons for his opposition to the American government. According to Aguinaldo, not only had the Americans humiliated his soldiers, but they were also treating the people of Manila abusively:

> In my manifesto of January 8 [1899], first I published the grievances suffered by the Philippine forces at the hands of the army of occupation. The constant outrages and taunts, which have caused the misery of the people of Manila, and finally, the useless conferences and the contempt shown the Philippine government provide the premeditated transgression of justice and liberty.

Needless to say, after centuries of domination by the Spanish, many Filipinos were not about to accept American colonization lying down, and they put their battle-hardened skills from fighting Spain to quick use, rushing against American forces in a frantic guerilla war. The result was war: brutal, devastating war. Slightly over half a year after the Americans put the final nail in the Spanish coffin in Manila Bay, the first fighting broke out between US forces and Aguinaldo's forces on the outskirts of Manila.

Emilio Aguinaldo. Image Credit: Wikimedia, Public Domain

Filipino independence fighters and insurgents continued what they regarded as keeping the Philippine Revolution going, except this time the rulers had a new flag. Even if the new invaders were American, it made little difference ideologically: the Filipino independence militias saw the Americans as illegitimate aggressors, and the American government saw the Philippines as a prime target for expansion and a worthwhile place to bolster America's economic and military reach.

Chapter 5 – February 4, 1899: War Breaks Out

The first shots of the Philippine-American War were fired on February 4, 1899. The American forces from the First Nebraska Regiment who were holding Manila began a firefight with a Filipino unit they spotted near their patrol zone. US Army Private William Grayson was patrolling when he reportedly saw Filipino fighters attempting to cross the San Juan Bridge onto American-held ground. Here, Grayson describes how he and another soldier began shooting at Filipinos near their patrol zone as a result of the incident:

> About eight o'clock, Miller and I were cautiously pacing our district. We came to a fence and were trying to see what the Filipinos were up to. Suddenly, near at hand, on our left, was a low but unmistakable Filipino outpost signal whistle. It was immediately answered by a similar whistle about twenty-five yards to the right. Then a red lantern flashed a signal from block-house number seven. We have never seen such a sign used before. In a moment, something rose up slowly in front of us. It was a Filipino. I yelled, "Halt!" and made it pretty loud, for I was accustomed to challenging the officer of the guard in approved military style. I challenged him with another loud "Halt!" Then he shouted "Halto!" to me. Well, I

> thought the best thing to do was to shoot him. He dropped. If I didn't kill him, I guess he died of fright. Two Filipinos sprang out of the gateway about fifteen feet from us. I called "Halt!" and Miller fired and dropped one. I saw that another was left. Well, I think I got my second Filipino that time.

The above passage displays the confusion of the war's beginning, as well as the cavalier American attitude regarding Filipinos as silly but dangerous pests. Alternate American sources than Grayson claim it was the Filipinos who fired first. Either way, two Filipinos are recorded as being killed in action that night, and sporadic fighting broke out along the line of contact.

Meanwhile, another American unit, under the leadership of Brigadier General Loyd Wheaton, took Pasig River. This cut Aguinaldo's forces in half across north and south Luzon, greatly hindering their ability to communicate across the lines going forward. Aguinaldo now had only a small path through American forces near Laguna de Bay, and his men south of Manila, in the most dedicated insurgent regions of Batangas, Laguna, and Cavite, were now stranded. General Antonio Luna served in the north, while Aguinaldo put Commander Mariano Trías in charge of the weakened south.

The southern American assault heading out of Manila, led by Major General Henry Lawton, was a minor success but didn't hold as much ground because of a lack of troops that had been devoted to the other two more important operations mentioned above. The Battle of Manila was intense but began to turn sharply into only one clear outcome: a decisive victory for the United States. It ended with 59 dead and 300 wounded Americans, and around 2,000 killed in action on the Filipino side with an unknown amount of injuries. The Americans, commanded by Major General Elwell Otis, had around 12,000 troops at the time and were facing off against more than 15,000 fighters on Aguinaldo's side.

The Filipinos lost the Battle of Manila badly, partly because February 5 was a Sunday, and many of the Filipino higher-ranking officers were attending Catholic Mass. Units were left in disarray, throwing a major wrench into their battle readiness and morale. As part of their system of patron-client relationships going back to Spanish colonial times, which impacted them both economically and militarily, the Filipinos were heavily reliant on their higher-ranking officers in the case of the military in order to uphold their reputation. A mentality of generally trying to save one's life rather than heroically fighting to the death prevailed among the ranks. Rather, the reigning idea at the start of the conflict was to fight hard as required but only up to a certain extent; once honor was preserved, they could then simply retreat. This was made all the more logical by the fact that the Filipinos were under-armed and often under-trained. American officers commented on the Filipinos' pattern of firing at the advancing American line and then systematically retreating when the US troops got to a few hundred yards, treating the war more as a kind of routine job than an all-out fight for their lives and independence.

General Gregorio del Pilar and his troops in Pampanga, around 1898. Image Credit: Public Domain

In either case, the Americans definitively crushed the Filipinos at Manila on February 5 and now controlled the surrounding terrain. The Filipino forces regrouped to make further decisions, with Aguinaldo in an increasingly precarious position as the leader because of his failure to come up with any effective victories against the Americans. The profile of General Luna continued to rise, worrying the paranoid Aguinaldo greatly.

As a young man, Luna had believed gradual reform was the best way to improve things for the Philippines, but he changed his views later after viewing the injustices of the Spanish and Americans. With a background in chemistry, literature, and fencing, Luna also became an accomplished sharpshooter, and he organized units that were nicknamed the "Luna Sharpshooters." Luna is widely regarded as one of the greatest military leaders during the war and even in the last few centuries, but his one shortcoming was a very bad temper. This divided people: they either loved him or despised him.

Luna had been deeply involved in the August 1898 Battle of Manila. He was angry about the Filipino troops being pushed aside by the Americans and ordered his men into the trenches to fire on the Americans. Although the official outbreak of the Philippine-American War would not be until 1899, the fact that Luna already saw the Americans as enemies demonstrates the stark divisions on the Filipino side from the very beginning.

To placate Luna, Aguinaldo kept promoting him until he was eventually made Supreme Chief of the Republican Army by September of 1898. Instead of being grateful, Luna was annoyed that he was being tossed ranks and ego-boosting titles instead of being allowed to turn the army into the fighting force he felt it should be. Eventually, he did start a military academy at Malolos—the forerunner to today's Philippine Military Academy—although it was paused by the time the war broke out with the United States. Luna also began publishing a newspaper called *La Independencia* (*The Independence*) in September, and it became a massive success with wide distribution among Filipinos.

Luna's mistrust of the Americans was vindicated when they fired on Filipino troops and began the war. Luna was closely involved in numerous high-stakes battles with the Americans and ordered his men that they pursue “war without quarter” for the Americans who “wish to enslave us.” Further explaining himself, Luna exclaimed, “Independence or death!” and said the Americans were rapists, thieves, and brigands who should never be trusted.

During the Battle of Santo Tomas in early May of 1899, Luna’s horse was shot out from under him as he charged the American lines. Laying on the ground, he realized he had been shot in the stomach. Luna was prepared to shoot himself in the head with his handgun so the Americans couldn’t capture him and extract information, but a colonel saw him fall and rescued him before he could kill himself.

By June of 1899, Luna was asked to go to the new Filipino capital at Cabanatuan and create a new government. After he got to Cabatuanan by June 5, Luna was walking up the stairway when he came across Captain Pedro Janolino from the Cavite Battalion, a man Luna had previously disciplined for failure to obey orders, and another man called Felipe Buencamino, Sr., the Philippine Republic’s minister of foreign affairs who had expressed support for American rule. They argued on the stairway about why Luna had been called there to meet Aguinaldo when he was not there, and a fight broke out. By the end, Luna had been stabbed and shot over forty times, and the men who had accompanied him were also killed under Aguinaldo’s orders as would later be revealed. “Cowards! Assassins!” Luna reportedly said in his dying breaths.

This didn’t happen until later in the war; Luna was still very much a part of the fighting for a few months more. For the next few months after the Americans took Manila, the American forces fought hard to crush the Filipino units across the island of Central Luzon, the biggest island in the Philippines. Digging trenches and marching through the jungle, the US troops engaged in sporadic and bloody fighting with the independence fighters, steadily depleting their ranks and causing them to begin engaging in some guerilla war tactics. The intensely humid climate and jungle conditions were new to most Americans, and in some cases, troops began suffering from severe exhaustion, dehydration, rashes, and blisters as the scorching sun beat down on them and the wet, hot jungle closed in.

When news of the outbreak of fighting in the Philippines got back stateside, politicians and the public were swept up in a buzz of patriotic fervor. The common sentiment was that all loyal Americans should "support our boys in the Philippines," and it even caused a partisan dispute with two Democrats leaving the party, as well causing the narrow victory of the yes vote to authorize the war in the Philippines. As such, the US Senate approved the terms of the Treaty of Paris by a vote of 57 to 27 on February 6, only two days after the fighting broke out in the Philippines. This meant the terms were passed by only one vote of the supermajority required for such a vote. The United States officially acquired the Philippines with President McKinley's signature on February 7, 1899.

As for the reaction domestically to the conflict, the media and intelligentsia were furious that America's largesse in bringing civilization to the Philippines was not being received with more gratefulness and acceptance. The American media, in particular, responded in full-on outrage, with the *New York Times* opining in February 1899 about "the insane attack of these people upon their liberators!" The editorial also expressed dismissal of the Filipino army's chances of posing any serious challenge to the superior American organization and firepower, writing that "it is not likely that Aguinaldo himself will exhibit much staying power. After one or two collisions, the insurgent army will break up."

Not for the first time, the *New York Times* was dead wrong.

Chapter 6 – Major Campaigns of the War

The Philippine-American War had two main stages of combat. The first, from the spring until the fall of 1899 (roughly February until November), was defined by Aguinaldo and the First Philippine Republic's hopeless scramble to fight the Americans head-on with conventional warfare tactics. The second stage of the war occurred after the re-election of President McKinley in November 1899 and lasted until the end of the war. The second stage was defined by the Filipino use of guerilla tactics and the worsening conditions and fighting practices against the civilian population.

In the conventional campaigns of the early war, the Filipinos were outgunned, outmaneuvered, and thoroughly routed. They simply could not fight the entrenched and dominant American military in a direct conventional fight and entered into a pattern of fight-retreat, fight-retreat, characterized by heavy casualties and constant losses. The United States military had much better weapons and equipment than the Filipinos and moved early to cut the Filipino supply routes and water access in order to cripple their ability to supply and reinforce their troops properly. Aguinaldo was also greatly disadvantaged by the refusal of outside powers to back him and his fighters. He and his men were essentially alone, with patchy support throughout the archipelago and a lack of enough ammunition, supplies, medical equipment, and proper training.

Filipino soldiers outside Manila, 1899. Image Credit: Public Domain.

Using guerilla warfare right from the very start could have put a much larger dent in the American forces. However, as it was used later, it merely extended the war and increased the atrocities on both sides as members of the United States military became enraged by what they perceived to be cowardly, "sneaky" fighting. Some soldiers began burning villages, as well as torturing and cutting off food supplies to geographical regions where they were unsure who was a fighter and who was a civilian. Although there is no evidence to suggest the US government ordered torture and civilian murder explicitly, extensive documentation shows that the American government largely turned a blind eye to it and mainly discounted the atrocities as the price of a hard-fought war. The Filipinos also engaged in atrocities, killing civilians who cooperated with Americans, torturing and dismembering US soldiers, and setting spike-filled booby traps hidden under foliage throughout the jungles that impaled and gruesomely killed American troops—reminiscent of future tactics that would be used by guerrilla armies, such as the Vietcong during the Vietnam War. The Filipino officer ranks were mainly trained to fight conventional wars, but they became convinced that there was no way to inflict serious damage on American troops by fighting conventionally. As they resorted to guerilla tactics more and more, the Americans became enraged at the "savage" tactics they associated with non-white peoples, further racializing the conflict.

As the fighting continued, America simultaneously began enacting its military governance model in the Philippines, which will be discussed in a future chapter. The process was implemented through successive governors, leading to the 1900 civilian leadership of future president William Howard Taft, who carried out a so-called "policy of attraction" characterized by the carrot or the stick philosophy. If they cooperated with the United States, they would get good schools, a strong economy, high-quality medical services, elections, municipal services, and a balanced legal system; however, if they went against the United States, they could only expect death and destruction. The strategy was fairly effective, particularly on an economic level and in terms of the argument that joining the United States would bring economic stability and opportunities, so many upper-class Filipinos and those who were not supporters of Aguinaldo began to come over to the American side covertly as well as overtly. Although this trend increased under the first civilian governor, William Howard Taft, it had begun as soon as the Americans became involved in the Philippines since various upper-class Filipinos saw the economic and social advantages of allying with the Americans right from the start.

In terms of the major campaigns of the war, stage one was characterized by conventional war, as aforementioned, and by early and decisive American troop movements to cut off, weaken, and decimate the Filipino fighters under Aguinaldo.

American troops marched on the large island of Luzon and deployed US ships full of soldiers to other heavily populated islands in an attempt to gain ground. Every time they made a full-frontal assault, the Filipinos retreated, but US soldiers were then butchered with surprise attacks from the jungle, and the guerilla tactics used changed the conflict for the Americans, reminding them of their last decades of counter-insurgency against Native Americans in the West of the United States. The war underwent a grim transformation into an unpredictable free-for-all, from the kind of standard unit-on-unit combat that had defined conflicts of the past century to a blitz-tactic guerilla war with no holds barred wholesale killing.

The Filipinos were fully committed to guerilla warfare against the Americans by the end of 1899. By the end of the year, the United States had 65,000 soldiers in the Philippines, determined to crush what they regarded as an unreasonable insurrection. As much as America may have half-stumbled into the annexation of the Philippines, it can certainly be said that it committed fully by the time it became clear that it would not be an easy war.

After the Americans successfully held Manila, the Filipinos saw that the fight against their new civilized adversaries would be a very difficult and sustained conflict. Major General Arthur MacArthur, Jr.—the father of the famous American General Douglas MacArthur, who became a Filipino hero for helping in their campaign against the occupying Japanese forces in the 1940s—was in charge of an American brigade asked to go on the attack on February 5, directly following the Battle of Manila, and headed out for a raid early in the morning.

The American strategy was to split in three directions— east, north, and south—to capture important Filipino depots in small villages. MacArthur's troops launched a strong attack on the village of Caloocan around a dozen miles north from Manila. Aguinaldo's troops had been displaced there following the Battle of Manila.

The battle before Caloocan, February 10, 1899 - View from the Chinese church. Maj. Gen. Arthur MacArthur on the inner wall, the battery of the Utah Artillery to the right of the church, the 10th Pennsylvania Volunteers of MacArthur's division in the middle foreground. Image Credit: Harper and Brothers, 1899, Public Domain

General MacArthur wanted to hit the Filipino defenders right after the battle of Manila on February 6 but was ordered by General Harrison Otis (not to be confused with the then commander of the American forces in the Philippines, Elwell Otis) to allow time for reinforcements and for the battle lines to shape up in a more clearly defined manner. By February 10, the attack went forward with a naval assault from the USS *Monadnock* and the USS *Charleston* and volleys from the 6th Artillery. MacArthur attacked Caloocan with his brigade, storming them at the central church and forcing the Filipinos to turn back and run toward the First Philippine Republic's capital of Malolos. Accusations of atrocities by some American soldiers arose after this battle, including Colonel W. Metcalfe who reportedly shot unarmed prisoners of war at Caloocan; he was covered for by Brigadier General Frederick Funston, who would go on to enthusiastically advocate war crimes as the only way to win the war. Metcalfe denied the accusations before Congress in a later testimony.

After heavy fighting, the Americans seized full control of Caloocan on February 10, locking down southern access to Dagupan railroad. With this move, they also gained one hundred freight railcars, fifty passenger railcars, and five train engines, which were a major boost to US logistical power and a major loss to Filipino operational ability and supply lines.

The ammunition train and reserves of the 20th Kansas Volunteers, Col. Frederick R. Funston, marching through Caloocan at night after the battle of February 10. Image Credit: Public Domain.

General Elwell Otis again wanted a slow advance following Caloocan instead of giving the green light to seize Malolos at the heart of the First Philippine Republic. Otis wanted the Filipinos to pour more resources and troops into the capital before the Americans came in to crush it.

Meanwhile, around two weeks later on February 22, the Filipinos tried to take back Caloocan in two days of sustained assaults. Led by General Luna, the Filipinos put great stock in the importance of this attempt to take back Caloocan, knowing that the result of the battle would make a large difference in their future battle preparedness and operational power. Planning at his base of operations in Valenzuela, General Luna split his men up into three fighting brigades—led by Colonel Maximino Hizon, General Mariano Llanera, and General Pantaleon Garcia—for a three-pronged attack strategy to retake Caloocan. The brigades had fairly high morale and were ready for action, with a well-developed plan to link up forces with the sympathizers still inside Manila while other fighting forces came to assist, with one led by General Licerio Gerónimo, coming from the east, and another led by General Miguel Malvar and Brigadier General Pío del Pilar from the south. Aguinaldo was not overly responsive to General Luna's requests for more men, but ultimately, General Luna was able to build up a combined troop strength surpassing 5,000 to fight against the 15,000 to 20,000 Americans on reserve in Manila and the surrounding area (about a six-hour march away from Caloocan).

The Filipinos set a start signal for themselves. It was activated once they lit a fire in a popular brothel in the Santa Cruz neighborhood of Manila on the night of February 22. The fire caused chaos in the city, and Filipino fighters stormed the north of the city, using the fire as cover. Colonel Francisco Román marched in and assaulted the shocked Americans later that night, but the Filipino side also had mixed signals and confusion in their ranks. Colonel Lucio Lucas—reporting directly to General Luna—had an operational snafu after trying to march immediately on a police station in downtown Manila, which had become an American military barracks, and ran into a strong American troop presence. With the fire to his back and armed Americans in the front, he ordered his under armed troops to advance. By the fight's end, three Filipinos and eight Americans were dead; apparently, the fire served as a good motivator to become highly committed to the battle.

On February 23, Filipino cannons launched volleys against Caloocan supported by infantry. Ammunition began to run low, causing stress and panic. There were also problems with communicating and coordinating with the sympathizers in Manila to launch a unified assault. Furthermore, the Filipinos advancing on Caloocan were met by a barrage from the USS *Monadnock*, which unleashed its considerable firepower of ten-inch shells on Filipino positions, devastating ranks and interrupting their artillery attack amid confusion and casualties.

General Garcia's troops had now entered Manila and were prepared to occupy their position to bolster the nearby attack on Caloocan when another Filipino unit ran into major trouble and set off a domino chain of disappointments. The big problem occurred when two Filipino companies of soldiers, led by Major Canlas, ran out of ammunition while besieging the city of La Loma, and almost one thousand men, totaling four companies from Cavite, were directed to go support them in order to oust the Americans from La Loma. Cavite's commanding officer, Captain Pedro Janolino, ignored the order, saying he would only listen to Aguinaldo, and La Loma was lost. Although Captain Janolino and his companies seized the Meisic barracks in Manila and the Filipinos managed to take Binondo, Sampaloc, and Tondo by nightfall on February 23, the loss of La Loma proved to be a crucial body shot for Filipino forces later in the war because of its strategic position and the amount of morale that the troops lost once the enemy gained it.

As the Filipinos led by Garcia and Llanera besieged Caloocan and its 6,000 American troops, the rest of the fighters rose for the day with renewed vigor and attacked Caloocan with gusto. The Americans were briefly worried but then settled back into their superior defensive positions and forced the Filipinos to repeatedly back down from their offensive strikes and regroup. The Americans destroyed the Filipino foothold in the Tondo area and eventually pushed the troops back from their attempt to retake Caloocan. General Luna's counterattack had failed, full stop. It was a devastating loss for the Filipinos' attempt to gain ground on the Americans. 39 Americans were listed as killed in action during the Second Battle of Caloocan, and 500 Filipino casualties were recorded.

General Luna was furious about Captain Janolino's refusal to obey him at La Loma and removed the Cavite Battalion of their weapons for Janolino's refusal to obey orders. Aguinaldo heard of General Luna's punishment and intervened, stripping him of his command and placing the Cavite Battalion under Major Ramos instead. Luna was devastated and resigned about a week later on February 28, although he was back fighting two weeks later. While Wheaton and Lawton were trying to gain ground in the surrounding areas of Caloocan and the Pasig River, as well as gaining a foothold in the south, General Elwell Otis executed an additional simultaneous campaign to gain more territory in Filipino strongholds. The **Iloilo Campaign**, lasting from February 8 to 12, set out to extend American power onto the surrounding Filipino islands from Luzon. Although Luzon was certainly the priority, the military understood that Aguinaldo's forces were retaining unchecked power on the other islands. The Americans moved to seize Panay Island, Cebu, Negros, and Jolo.

The city of Iloilo on Panay Island fell to the fierce American assault led by General Marcus Miller, who had valuable naval support from Captain Frank Wilde. Filipino General Martín Delgado simply could not prevent the devastating American combined land and air attacks that left the city a burnt-out husk, with torched buildings and bombarded shells that had been due to Wilde's warships. American troops marched in to take control of Iloilo on February 11, setting it up as an important outpost of island power for the United States.

Troops seized the capital city of Cebu after a long attack with US naval support. Rear Admiral Dewey sent Captain Charles Cornwell and his ship, the *Petrel*, to attack Cebu's main port on February 21.

It was taken by February 26, with the reinforcing American troops, led by Major Greenleaf Goodale from the 23rd Infantry, marching in by mid-March to hold the line. Lieutenant Colonel Thomas Hamer became the military governor of the Cebu portion of the Visayas District.

The city of Bacolod on the island of Negros crumbled under the American offensive on March 10, with American Brigadier General James Smith taking charge as the military governor of Negros.

Jolo was under American control by May 19.

The **Malolos Campaign** began on March 24 when Major General MacArthur marched north along the Ferrocarril de Manila-Dagupan railway to advance on the First Philippine Republic's capital of Malolos and destroy the independence fighters. General Elwell Otis had divided the 8th Corps into two parts: one to guard Manila against attack and the other, MacArthur's, to strike at Aguinaldo's capital.

Major General MacArthur diversified his assault, sending one brigade north up the railway and another across the Quingua River and down a small local road. At the Battle of the Tuliahan River on March 25, the Americans faced heavy resistance on a well-defended Filipino stronghold and were temporarily slowed down. The next day, American troops came out guns blazing after emerging from the combat at the river, progressing north and gunning down around one hundred Filipino soldiers at the Battle of Meycauayan Bridge.

Elsewhere on the same day of March 26, 1899, American troops were ambushed in the village of Malinta. After finding it abandoned, they thought they were in the clear only to be assailed from all sides by hidden Filipino soldiers. American Captain John Ballance confronted the assault and gained the rank of lieutenant colonel for helping the Americans get away with few casualties and driving the Filipinos back.

The following day at the Battle of Marilao River, US troops managed to cross the 80-yard-wide Marilao River under heavy enemy fire, which in retrospect was seen as a great victory and a heroic moment in the Philippine-American War. It was in heavy contrast to the Battle of Bocaue River several days later on March 29, where American troops were mowed down halfway during their attempt to cross the river and absorbed 29 casualties in a ten-minute span.

Major General MacArthur's brigade marching on Malolos arrived at the end of March only to find that Aguinaldo and his army had left the capital behind, switching their capital and center of military operations to San Fernando, which was about a three-hour march away.

General Elwell Otis had sent Major General Lawton west to block the Filipino troops, but Lawton ordered his men to Norzagaray in the north in order to lure the Filipino troops away from their defense of General Luna's main base at Calumpit, a heavily bolstered fort of steel-reinforced infrastructure defended by around 7,000 soldiers in the surrounding area. On April 10, General Luna went after the advancing Americans, inflicting heavy casualties, but he did not manage to defeat them. With MacArthur's men combined with Lawton's 1st Brigade and Brigadier General Irving Hale's 2nd Brigade, Calumpit fell on April 25 as the Americans fought on past the initial shock of Luna's heavy defenses and over 4,000 soldiers.

Meanwhile, Brigadier General Wheaton's troops had been engaging in heavy combat as they made their way along various rivers up to Laguna de Bay during the month of March, eventually shearing Aguinaldo's army in half between north and south. While MacArthur's men fought in the north, Brigadier General Henry Lawton's troop column headed south, capturing Santa Cruz in the Laguna de Bay region on the island of Luzon, including Pagsanjan on April 11 and Paete on April 12. Lawton and his men headed back victorious to Manila by April 17. Lawton was confident in pushing farther on Luzon and taking Calamba but was recalled by General Otis, leading to the recapture of Santa Cruz by the Filipinos. Instead, Lawton was sent to Quingua.

On April 23, American reconnaissance scouts around Quingua were spotted and were under heavy fire from Filipino troops, so General Otis ordered Lawton's troops to take Quingua, which fell on April 24. The fighting was intense, with American artillery pounding the town to smithereens and infantry troops assaulting heavily defended enemy lines. The Americans lost a high-ranking officer in the battle as well, Colonel John Stotsenburg. The acquisition of Quingua was an enormous boost in helping the Americans seize General Luna's stronghold of Calumpit after a day of intense, bloody fighting on April 25.

By early May, Aguinaldo sent delegates to ask for a three-week truce and to recognize the legal validity of the First Philippine Republic as an independent nation under international law. He was turned down by General Elwell Otis, who provided them with the details of President McKinley's blueprint for Filipino governance, which included input and decision-making from the Filipinos. The representatives were convinced, and Aguinaldo's war cabinet was turned upside down, electing Pedro Paterno—at the time a diplomat who advocated a ceasefire with the Americans—in order to discuss surrender with General Harrison Otis. Hearing of this development, General Luna detained Aguinaldo's delegates and Paterno's peace cabinet members and put those who favored the war back in place. The war was back on.

On May 4, the United States seized San Fernando, but they were having major supply and logistics issues because of how far north MacArthur's men had moved since February. The troops were sick and exhausted. They used the rest of May to take a break in San Fernando and get ready for the next phase of the battle.

MacArthur's men had taken Malolos on March 31, 1899, without any resistance, although retreating Filipinos under General Luna's command torched the buildings in order to starve Americans of resources and fortified positions. After seizing Malolos, the Americans used it to help seize Angeles, which was taken on August 16, 1899—the conclusion of the Malolos campaign.

The first **San Isidro Campaign** took place between April 21 and May 30, 1899. It included the capture of Calumpit and Major General Lawton's successful seizure of San Rafael, Baliuag, and Bustos by May 2. The taking of Baliuag was especially significant as it led to Lawton's issuance on May 7 of General Field Order 8 that authorized a local US-supported government. It allowed the locals to elect a mayor and council to lead their town and run their municipal affairs. The San Isidro campaign continued with the capture of San Miguel by May 16 and San Isidro which began on May 16 and ended on May 17 with an American victory. The Battle for San Isidro is recorded as having begun after American reconnaissance scouts came across Filipino troops torching a bridge to prevent any future crossings. Four American scouts—recognizing the logistical crippling that such a move would accomplish—stormed the Filipinos, who fled as the rest of the scouts forded the crossing and doused the bridge with water to save it. This was key, as it allowed US troops the next day to cross the bridge and seize San Isidro. Unluckily for the Americans, Aguinaldo knew of their advance well ahead of time, and his fighters and intermediate government had taken up and run away to Tarlac, along with thirteen American prisoners of war.

June saw the fierce **Battle of Zapote River**, which erupted in one single angry clash on June 13, 1899. It was monsoon season in the summer of 1899, and military maneuvers had largely stopped due to the torrents of rain. The Americans used the pause to bring in fresh troops, establishing the Philippine Scouts and upping the strength of the 8th Army Corps to around 50,000 by that summer and 75,000 by 1900. During the one remarkable battle during this time of replenishing troops, Major General Lawton's troops fought a unit commanded by Brigadier General Pío del Pilar at the Zapote River. The battle was especially important because it routed the Filipinos and led them back to focusing almost completely on guerilla tactics instead of the kind of direct fighting that always seemed to lead to their defeat, even when they had superior numbers.

A group of Filipino insurgents is photographed just as they lay down their weapons prior to surrender. Original caption is "Prayer Before the Surrender." 1900. Image Credit: Philippines War Dept.

Lawton brought around 1,200 US troops while del Pilar's forces numbered approximately 5,000. The Zapote River is located on the island of Luzon in between Bacoor in the Cavite province to the south and the village of Las PiÑas and the capital of Manila northward. Its wreckage is still visible today for interested visitors, and a new bridge was built near it on the Philippine's Aguinaldo Highway. The brick bridge had been the location of a fierce fight in 1897 during the Philippine Revolution to oust Spain, and once again, it would play a role in the Philippine-American War.

US gunboats led by Rear Admiral George Dewey backed up the infantry on land and were joined by four more powerful gunboats soon after. Fighting broke out in the early morning around 6 a.m. on June 13 when American reconnaissance troops scouting the area took fire from the Filipinos. The Americans returned fire, while soldiers from the 21st Infantry came up against almost 1,000 Filipinos nearby, who were armed with rifles and some artillery. The US troops began to run out of ammunition and ran for cover to the beach, where backup troops came in. Gunboats *Helena* and

Monadnock positioned themselves for support and unloaded more infantry.

US forces under Brigadier General Sam Ovenshine and First Lieutenant William Kenly advanced the attack on the bridge, picking off the Filipinos with targeted fire. The bridge was heavily damaged and couldn't be used to cross. Fighting spread all the way to the beach where the recovering troops were resting. US gunboats littered the shore with devastating shell attacks, killing dozens of Filipino troops in blood-spattered carnage. By late afternoon, around 5 p.m., the Filipinos retreated, and the US forces patched up the bridge to cross, with Brigadier General Wheaton and Major General Lawton leading the efforts. The Americans sent troops forward and found more Filipinos holding out south of the bridge and scattered them, while defensive fighting from other Filipino forces delayed the Americans long enough for the bulk of the Filipino force to retreat to safety and flee.

The fighting killed 150 Filipinos and injured 375 and killed 15 Americans and injured 75. American Captain William Sage was given the Medal of Honor for his bravery during combat. It was an absolute bloodbath and the second largest battle in the entire war after the first Battle of Manila.

Hostilities between the Americans and the Filipinos were now at an all-time high and would not abate for several years. Filipino fighters used guerilla tactics, disguising themselves in civilian populations, striking US forces hard at night when they were asleep, and making bloody traps in the jungle. In his June 1899 "Proclamation of War" around four months into the conflict, Filipino politician Pedro Paterno—who had initially urged diplomacy with the Americans—said all blame for the war lay on the United States, expressing the Filipino point of view and narrative about the war:

> No one is ignorant of the fact that since we took the direction of the Ship of State we have sacrificed ourselves to the services of the government of our republic, offering

ourselves as victims for the sake of peace without abandoning the sacred idea of liberty and independence which fires our country; but the North Americans refuse to suspend hostilities, asked for by us so that we may consult the National Assembly, seat of free popular sovereignty. The Commissioners returning from Manila so declare.

Since it is their desire, may the responsibility of the war and its consequences fall on the great nation of the United States of America.

We have done our duty as patriots and human beings, showing the great powers of the world that the present cabinet has the diplomacy necessary to protect our cause as well as the arms required to defend our rights.

The Council of Government, deciding to preserve our republican institutions, national independence, and the presidency of Don Emilio Aguinaldo, in spite of the Americans, who intended to construct upon our ruins the edifice of tyranny, has concluded to continue the war, preserving unhurt in their spirit and letter our constitution and laws, which we have conquered with so much blood and such sacrifices.

To war, then, beloved brothers, to war!

In order that the people be free it is necessary that they be brave. Rich and poor, learned and ignorant, beloved Filipinos, hasten to unite to save our native land from insult and ignominy, from punishments and scaffolds, from the sad and fatal inheritance of enslaved generations. The God of War, in whom we have put our faith and hope, will help us.

Confusion, internal and international dissensions and conflicts, rend the invading army; its volunteers, being aware that we are in the right, fight without enthusiasm and only in compliance with their forced military duty. Within the

> American nation itself, a great political party asks for the recognition of our rights, and the Divine Providence watches over the justice of our case.

It is clear from Paterno's tone that the Filipinos held a great deal of idealism but also considerable bitterness about the actions of the Americans for going back on their word when it came to Philippine independence, at least not beyond limited local Filipino governance as instituted, for example, on Negros.

Chapter 7 – America's Military Government in the Philippines

As the United States worked to defeat Filipino resistance militarily, it also worked to put in place institutions and structures that would steadily bring over non-combatants and wealthy members of society to their vision for the future of the Philippines. As part of the military occupation, the military governor was tasked with the overall mission of bringing the Philippines in line with American ambitions. Beginning with Major General Wesley Merritt in 1898, the position then transferred to General Elwell Otis later that year, who held it until 1900 when the title shifted to Major General Arthur MacArthur. He held it until 1901, and thereafter, it was shared from 1901 to 1902 between civilian Governor-General and future POTUS William Howard Taft and well-recognized military general Adna Chaffee. Under Taft's oversight, the Philippines truly shifted into a testing ground for Progressive Era initiatives, instituting Western educational curricula, English language lessons, and laws that cracked down on anti-American sentiments expressed through any form of Filipino culture, including music, art, and literature. Taft thoroughly shared the predominant view of the Filipinos as being backward, childlike people in need of Anglo-Saxon rule, telling President McKinley that "our little brown brothers" would require up to one hundred years of "close supervision" in order to cultivate "anything resembling Anglo-Saxon political principles and skills."

Under American direction, a number of municipal governments were set up and staffed by Filipinos who supported the American mission. The American strategy in this regard was to basically fill the positions with individuals from the upper class of the Philippines, known as the *Ilustrados*, as well as to split the local populations by ethnic divisions that had been longstanding and bitter prior to American arrival. This, similar to the British colonial strategy in India and other locales, was actually quite effective, as it prevented a critical mass of Filipinos from unifying and led to a considerable number joining the American military government. The Filipinos did so both for the benefits and power that it could confer and because of a lack of feelings of solidarity or trust for Filipinos of other ethnicities and classes who were ostensibly their countrymen. Military Governor Elwell Otis believed that dislike of the majority Tagalog ethnicity—of which Aguinaldo was a part—would allow the Americans to install rival and disloyal governments across the islands, which they did do on the island of Negros, Central Luzon, and the Muslim region of Sulu.

The American goal with the military government was to make the Philippines learn the American way of doing things. Leading American statesmen, like John Barrett, stated the belief that with American help, the Filipinos would eventually be ready for freedom and "all the privileges of absolute independence." The US Congress had not formally set out regulations for how to manage the islands, and so, the American forces retained many previous regulations and systems that Spain had used. Taxation, the postal system, courts, local law enforcement, and marriage were all run by the US military, which had authority to delegate as it saw fit. The military mainly filled positions with National Guardsmen and members of the US Army who had experience in such jobs prior to their enlistment.

There were few restrictions on the military's leeway to do as it saw fit, although President McKinley did announce that the Filipinos were "entitled to security in their persona and property and in all their private rights and relations" as long as they complied with American directions and did not engage in any fighting against the United States.

As part of its goal of setting up rivals and alternatives to the First Philippine Republic and Aguinaldo's Tagalog-dominated government, the army put out General Order (GO) no. 30 in 1899, which set up a relatively open military government on Negros in the Visayan island chain. This order was followed by additional GOs that sent junior officers to implement the American system and allowed them to institute martial law during uprisings. American civilian leadership was working to take over in some cases as a counterbalance to military rule, and the governor-general of the Philippines, William Howard Taft, was put in charge, basically transferring over many military functions into civil control under his purview. By 1901, the control began to shift, although the military stayed in charge of towns and islands where there were heavier fighting and resistance, eventually leading to the creation of concentration camps for civilians set up by Brigadier General James Franklin Bell near the end of the war, particularly in southern Luzon.

Freedom under the military government was granted to a certain degree as long as the locals were agreeable and followed American orders. Many everyday positions were run by Filipinos and overseen by American soldiers and military authorities. Although the Americans demanded the right to run the islands, they did not want to formally "own" them or grant statehood to the Philippines because of the perception that a non-white and "uncivilized" people would be absurd to include within the Union. For this reason, provisions under the 1787 Northwest Ordinance Act as to including new land in the nation was sidestepped by Congress. Instead, they issued a resolution sponsored by Senator Samuel McEnery which granted Filipinos different and lesser rights than American citizens. Their argument for this eventually came down to a number of tariff regulations. If tariffs and tariff restrictions could be placed on a US-controlled territory, then it was outside the Constitution's jurisdiction, and so, the Bill of Rights also did not apply. Anti-imperialist politicians, like William Jennings Bryan and Senator George Frisbee Hoar, were worried about what annexing a nation without fully incorporating it would do for future situations. They were worried that this kind of double-talk could essentially accomplish backdoor imperialism, but pro-imperialist politicians and forces won the day.

The Office of the Secretary of War and the Spooner Amendment in 1901 also confirmed the US government's legal "right" to rule the Philippines without legally incorporating it into the United States. This prompted angry reactions from anti-imperialists, but it still stood, ensuring that the military and the president had enormous power and self-justification in their actions in the Philippines.

If locals or local leaders resisted or caused problems, President McKinley made it clear that the military could "replace or expel native officials in part or altogether" if necessary. Starting with the military government set up in Manila in the summer of 1898 just prior to the start of the war, the American military set up a tight system of control, which was partly aimed at gaining the loyalty of the upper classes and ensuring a flow of food and supplies to stop the hungry and frustrated inhabitants from defecting to Aguinaldo. Roles were delegated, including that of a provost marshal to institute martial law after the war started, and an American force was soon set up to replace the police. American military control came in handy early on when Filipino rebels tried to raze Manila shortly after the start of the war on February 15. They were stopped, but they were still able to torch half a million US dollars of goods and property—an enormous sum of money in those times.

From the beginning, the military government boosted infrastructure, healthcare, and public services, including immunization programs. It even went so far as to develop a system of testing and certifying prostitutes in order to declare them free from venereal diseases, in no small part motivated by the American soldiers' use of those women. The Americans in charge also put in place an immigration prohibition on the Chinese in order to act in the interests of the Filipino working class, whose jobs were being taken away by Chinese immigrants who became prosperous merchants and created trade monopolies. The US ran the customs system as well, gathering major revenues from it and securing an economic foothold in vital areas, especially in regards to Manila's trade flow.

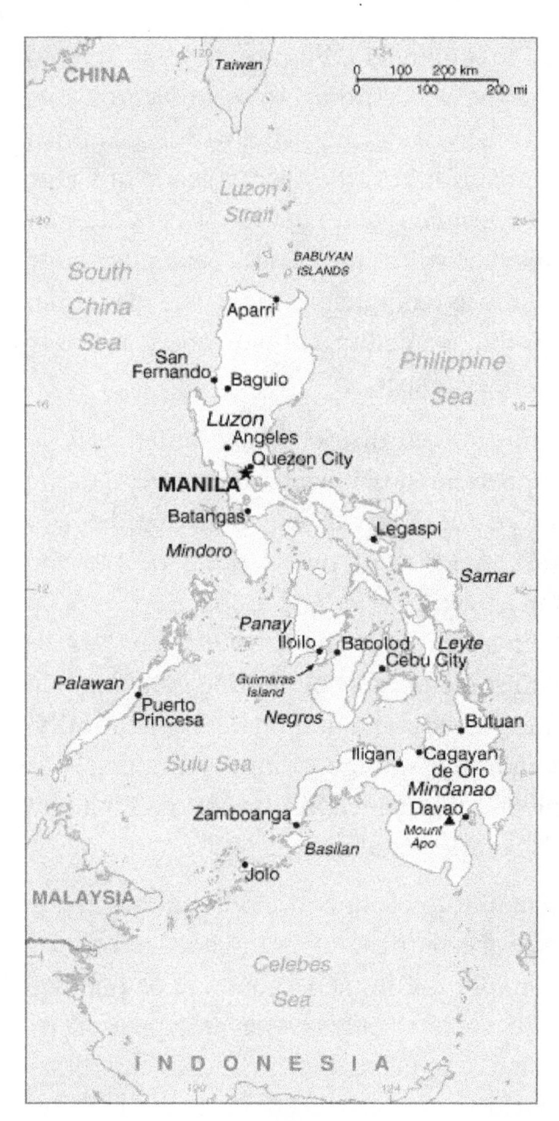

Detailed Map of the Philippines. Image Credit: Public Domain

Manila was basically the beta test of the military governance across the islands, and it worked fairly well, leading to the establishment of a representative local government on Negros and its Visayan ethnicity. The Visayans hated Aguinaldo and the Tagalog group and were thus a logical choice for the Americans to install a government, which they had the luxury of allowing to remain somewhat free since it was already opposed to Aguinaldo. Filipino fighters loyal to Aguinaldo had been crossing the water from Luzon to Negros, and the *Ilustrados* and ruling class there were angry and worried. For that reason, they invited the Americans in. On the nearby island of Cebu, the US Navy ran the local government and kept the waters clear of pirates and rebel deployments, with the locals generally quite supportive of their efforts. It was completely night and day from Luzon, where most of the people wanted to kill the Americans or at the very least were neutral on the subject.

Voting in the American-administrated districts was limited only to the landowning *Ilustrados* upper class, who were male, over 21, and literate in English, Spanish, or the Visayan language. Needless to say, this eliminated the vast majority of the working people and simple farmers. Smaller towns on Negros and Cebu were run by mostly independent local governments. The situation on Negros remained relatively calm with some pockets of fighting breaking out. Nonetheless, Negros became increasingly important economically, with new sugar mills and industry springing up. An election was successfully held in November 1899, which also marked a highlight of the military government's soft power abilities.

Starting in Manila and expanding to more and more regions, many *Ilustrados* simply did not see the purpose of independence or very much care about it. It was simply not in their economic or political interests. Many business and societal elites were unimpressed by Aguinaldo and the Katipunan's requests for financial and other support. This attitude is perfectly encapsulated in a public letter made by Jose Basa, a rich Filipino expatriate residing in Hong Kong at the time of Dewey's defeat of the Spanish at Manila Bay in 1898. Basa was overjoyed and rejected the idea that the Philippines should continue in any way with their quest for independence, writing that American rule was "the best opportunity" the islands had ever had and that accepting their leadership would lead to the Philippines being "rich, civilized and happy." Basa was far from alone in his view, which was yet another thing that greatly crippled Aguinaldo's attempt in his fight for independence.

The upper class of the Philippines, some of whom had left during the conflict with Spain, wanted what was best for business. In order to gain some of their loyalty to his cause, Aguinaldo—himself from a very rich, aristocratic family—handed high positions in his government to any *Ilustrado* who would come on board, even if they were clearly underqualified. The remainder of the upper classes—those living abroad and those who were still residing in the islands—preferred to remain either neutral or at least gradually warming to the idea of American rule.

Giving the Filipinos some limited self-government made the Americans feel both justified and more confident about the war, particularly as its bloodier episodes and battles began emerging to the forefront. Using both reward and punishment, the military government slowly built on the existing Spanish structure and successfully instituted some colonial government structures, setting the foundation for the later systems which would prevail in the Philippines. The American system also focused on taking power out of Manila and instead delegating it to elites and *Ilustrados* in the different provinces who could help uphold American interests, motivating these individuals to seek more and more friendships with American government interests in order to advance their own interests and commercial success.

Chapter 8 – Escalation: The Naval Blockade and Fierce American Campaigns

Determined to do whatever was necessary to win the war, the United States put in place a full naval blockade on the Philippines on August 19, 1899. All trade and transfer of any supplies or weapons were fully barred. Ordered by Rear Admiral John Watson, the blockade was enforced by two dozen US gunboats and almost one dozen army river steamers set up to block access to Cebu, Iloilo, Vigan, Zamboanga, Jolo, and Siassi. The blockade certainly had an effect and began to hurt the already shaky Filipino supply lines even further.

The war dragged on across the islands, leading to the important **Cavite Campaign** in the fall between October 7 and 13. The week of fighting was brought about after Major General Henry Lawton, Colonel William Bisbee, and Brigadier General Theodore Schwan led an advance on pockets of fierce Filipino insurgency in Cavite.

As the Americans battled the Filipinos across the islands, Filipino troops began attacking south of Manila in Los BaÑos, Imus, Bacoor, and Calamba in the Cavite region as 1899 progressed. General Elwell Otis—who wanted all possible troops for the northward assaults he was focused on—moved decisively to crush the southern fighters, sending troops westward along Manila Bay, another along Laguna de Bay, and a third naval-supported column to Noveleta. The Americans won decisively in all of these campaigns.

The Macabebe Scouts. Image Credit: Wikimedia, Public Domains.

The **Second San Isidro Campaign** took place around the same time but lasted for longer, going from October 10 to November 20, 1899. Major General Lawton's troops moved up Pampanga River and retook San Isidro by October 20 with a brigade under the leadership of Brigadier General Samuel Young and First Lieutenant Matthew Batson's Philippine Scouts (also known as the Macabebe Scouts). Unlike American society, which was firmly moving toward securing segregation and implementing a racial hierarchy, Batson saw the potential and humanity of the Filipinos, learning the Pampangan language from a servant called Jacinto whom Batson met soon after arriving. In return, Batson taught Jacinto English and learned that Jacinto came from the Macabebe tribe, long-time enemies of the Tagalogs who lived to the northwest of Manila. All of this helped lead to Batson's creation of the Philippine Scouts, which proved to be successful and helped rally support for the American side among some of the local non-Tagalog population.

After gaining San Isidro with the help of the Philippine Scouts, Brigadier General Young ordered his troops north to Cabanatuan, where upward of two dozen American and 4,000 Spanish prisoners of war were allegedly being held. The trek was very difficult over the rugged terrain, but it resulted in a successful seizure of the city. Young then moved on with a cavalry brigade, which was over 1,000 strong, and attacked San Jose, capturing it on November 12 and Umangan on November 13. Tayug and San Nicholas soon followed on November 16 and San Fernando de la Union fell on November 20. Other Americans troops had also taken San Fabian in the Pangasinan province by November 18.

The **Tarlac Campaign** around the same period in the fall of 1899 was a ferocious confrontation that lasted from around November 5 to 20. The fighting occurred along the Central Luzon plain and resulted in the seizure of Tarlac on November 12 and the American forces taking Dagupan by November 20. The campaign started when Major General MacArthur's troops, along with those of Colonel Jacob Smith and the 17th Infantry, the 36th Infantry under Brigadier General James Franklin Bell, and the 9th and 12th Infantries under Brigadier General Joseph "Fighting Joe" Wheeler, started advancing from Angeles toward the municipality of Bamban in Tarlac. Although they seized Bamban on November 12 and were about to head for their next target, the weather had other plans. Along the way, there was a massive storm, and a river flooded, eroding roadways and making transport impossible. Troops repaired the roads for around four days and waited until the supplies caught up to them before going on to take over Bayambang by November 19 and then Dagupan by November 20, signaling the end of the campaign.

In the same timeframe, the **San Fabian Campaign** took place, lasting from November 6 to 19 with Major General Loyd Wheaton's, Colonel William Bisbee's, and Colonel Luther Hare's troops deploying on November 7 at San Fabian after embarking by boat from Manila. They continued on to confront Filipino fighters at San Jacinto on November 11, where Major General Wheaton's troops successfully routed the Filipinos and sent them scrambling out of San Jacinto. American troops from the San Fabian campaign eventually reached Dagupan in a joint operation with MacArthur's troops, taking the city together by November 20.

On December 4, Colonel Hare's 220-strong fighting force from the 33rd Infantry marched south, and the men of the 34th Infantry marched north, liberating over 200 Spanish and two dozen American prisoners of war. Later that December, in Cagayan Valley, there was also an important milestone in the war when American Commander Bowman McCalla forced the surrender of Filipino soldiers under Daniel Tirona at Cagayan Valley on December 11.

Later, on December 19, the **Battle of Paye** was fought in Luzon, leading to the killing of Major General Henry Lawton by Filipino troops in the Morong Command and its *Tiradores de la Muerte* (Shooters of Death) under the command of General Licerio Gerónimo. The battle took place near San Mateo in the Rizal province, although in December of 1899, it was part of the Manila province. On the day of December 18, Major General Lawton and his soldiers were headed to San Mateo along the Marikina River, where they hoped to catch Brigadier General del Pilar's 1,000-men fighting force and decimate it. Del Pilar's troops were a danger to the Marikina water system, and they also had the road north to Manila blocked. Major General Lawton had a large force, including Colonel James Lockett's 11th Cavalry and Lieutenant Colonel H. Sargent's 29th Battalion.

Heavy rains had flooded out the Marikina River, making the American advance very difficult, although they managed to seize the town of Montalban by December 19, with Sargent's men advancing in a pincer move to come at San Mateo. As the attack on San Mateo got underway, the well-organized Filipinos pinned Lawton and his men down in rice paddies with heavy fire and prevented their easy access to San Mateo. The Americans were taking huge casualties and were being killed and injured left, right, and center. Major General Lawton was rallying his troops along the frontline when a Filipino sniper named Bonifacio Mariano hit him with a shot to the chest. Following this, Sargent found a ford in the river and repulsed the Filipino defenders out of San Mateo to successfully capture the city.

Forty Americans were killed in action during the Battle of Paye and 125 injured, while 11 Filipinos were killed and 13 injured. The killing of Major General Lawton marked the highest rank to die in the war on the American side, and the news was devastating to his troops and the American public. Lawton is buried at Arlington National Cemetery, and many places honor his service by using his name (Fort Lawton and Lawton, Oklahoma, being a few examples). Writing of the Filipinos before his death in a letter, Major General Lawton bucked the trend of dismissing them as savages or heathens, saying that their major disadvantages in terms of ammunition, supplies, weapons, and organization were offset by their determination. "They are the bravest men I have ever seen," Lawton wrote.

The fighting continued in January of 1900 with General Elwell Otis' attempt to capture the southern regions of the Philippines. The January 18 to 27 Hemp Expedition, by Brigadier General William Kobbé and Commodore Raymond Rogers, seized ports that traded in abaca (a species of banana that is often called Manilla hemp), as well as Sorsogon City, Calbayog, Catbalogan, Tacloban, and Ormoc.

However, the tides would not always remain in favor of the US forces. The Siege of Catubig, lasting from April 15 to 19, 1900, was notable in that it saw Filipino troops launch a devastating surprise attack on the Americans and forced them to retreat, and the Battle of Makahambus Hill on June 4, 1900, in northern Mindanao also resulted in a rare Filipino victory against the Americans when they filleted the American ranks and caused a huge amount of casualties but took almost none among their men. The Battle of Pulang Lupa on September 13, 1900, where Filipino troops led by Colonel

Maximo Abad blindsided a force of Americans under Captain Devereux Shields on the island of Marinduque. Furthermore, the Battle of Mabitac on September 17, 1900, was yet another battle where the Filipinos crushed American forces, this time on Luzon at Mabitac.

Chapter 9 – The War Hits Home

As new American troops poured in during the summer of 1900, opposition grew back in the United States, which had already been politically divided over the question of the Philippines in the first place. Casualty rates had climbed much higher than the Americans were expecting, with a total of 3,000 American dead and 15,000 Filipino fighters killed in action by that point. It was far from a minor skirmish, and President McKinley was faced with considerable pressure about how to deal with the fallout. In an attempt to offset public alarm, bad news from the Philippines began being censored by that summer, with war reporters required to submit their work for review. Members of the media were considerably disappointed and angry, but they generally blamed American military leadership for the censorship rules rather than blaming President McKinley.

Groups like the Anti-Imperialist League were leading the opposition against the war, and politicians like William Jennings Bryan and public figures like author Mark Twain also highlighted their belief in the war's barbarity and senselessness. As Twain put it, "I am opposed to having the eagle put its talons on any other land." The Anti-Imperialist League, a group that was founded by traditional and anti-war Americans to oppose American military interventionism and global engagements, advanced a partly socially conservative argument against the war, saying that it was spreading venereal disease and exposing troops to loose women and prostitutes, as well as irresponsible amounts of drinking and the encouragement of their baser instincts which led to violence and killing.

Around 1900, the Filipinos had lost much of their fighting organization and morale. The United States believed the war was basically over but was summarily faced with reinvigorated fighting during that spring. Divided into over 450 bases scattered across the islands, the American forces combed through the jungle, looking for Filipino fighters, and worked to control and subdue villagers and buy their loyalty through force or persuasion. America worked to pacify the people, build up local services, and improve schools in order to get the villagers and upper classes on their side, as detailed by authors like John Gates in his book, *Schoolbooks and Krags*. Gates even called the war an example of "enlightened military government," dismissing concerns that it was overly brutal, racist, or harsh. While many historians have depicted Gates as being overly optimistic and whitewashing in his account of American actions, other authors, like Leon Wolff in *Little Brown Brother*, have talked of the war's horrors and details the American atrocities against civilians, which were spurred by racism and the lack of discipline.

American troops were increasingly enraged by the open-ended conflict and the brutal tactics being used by Filipino troops, which included traps in the jungle and ambush sniper attacks. A soldier by the name of A.A. Barnes wrote that after one of their men was found eviscerated and cut open with his guts strewn all over, the troops were ordered to torch the village and kill any Filipino they saw. Barnes lamented in a letter that he had become "hard-hearted" because he admitted he loved the feeling of gunning down any Filipino he saw, writing that "I am in my glory when I can sight my gun on some dark skin and pull the trigger."

The modern rights of soldiers and civilians in wars came about through the 1862 writings of Swiss peace proponent and Red Cross founder Henry Dunant, who spoke of the need for a neutral body that would uphold rights in war and prosecute those who violated them. During his acceptance of the controversially awarded Nobel Peace Prize in 2009, former US President Barack Obama—a leader who frequently used drone strikes that killed many innocent civilians—spoke of the need to revere Dunant for the work he had done. There have been four Geneva Conventions establishing human rights and rules of war; they were signed in 1864, 1906, 1929, and 1949, respectively, and there were also internationally agreed-upon rights during war that were signed in the Hague Conventions in 1899 and 1907. The Hague Conventions were mainly based on what is called the Lieber Code, which had been signed by President Abraham Lincoln during the US Civil War in 1863 in order to try to stop the atrocities being committed against Southerners by the Union Army. The Geneva rules, for their part, put in place obligations that governments would agree to as to how to treat prisoners of war, how to treat wounded enemy combatants, the use of torture, civilian rights in a warzone, and numerous other matters. It is worth noting that the first 1864 Geneva Convention had been signed by twelve nations by the time of the Philippine-American War.

By June 1900, when Republicans met for the Republican National Convention in Philadelphia, the war had not dragged down President McKinley's re-nomination, and he easily won due to the economic boom that was going on at the time in the United States following the major economic recession of the 1890s. The re-election ticket was beefed up with Theodore Roosevelt—who had ordered the fortuitous naval attack on Manila Bay and was a popular war hero from leading the famous Rough Riders cavalry unit during the Spanish-American War—as McKinley's running mate.

The presidential election of 1900 was once again McKinley against William Jennings Bryan, an anti-interventionist populist who wanted to bring the issue of the war into the center of American public attention and highlight the abuses and horrors occurring in order to explain why the United States had no business—nor real interest—in being an empire. Despite a solid core of supporters and a significant segment of public opinion on his side, Bryan was unsuccessful. Voters loved the booming economy, and the majority favored the idea of bringing the Philippines to heel and subduing its "uncivilized" and backward people.

By October 1901, the difficulty in fighting an insurgent force and US anger led to undeniable war crimes. Brigadier General Jacob Smith infamously ordered his troops to "kill and burn" on the island of Samar after over forty US troops were killed. He reportedly said he wanted the entire island turned into a "howling wilderness." According to Smith's orders, anyone over the age of ten should be shot on sight, regardless of their apparent hostility or combatant status. As a veteran of fighting the Native Americans, including the massacre at Wounded Knee, Smith was a grizzled killer who had no interest in soft-pedaling the conflict or talking about treating the Filipinos humanely. He remarked in 1899 to reporters that the Filipinos were worse than the "savages" he'd fought in the United States and that they deserved and required the same scorched-earth tactics and all-out destruction. William Howard Taft's co-governor of the Philippines, Adna Chaffee, expressed the feelings of many when he wrote that those the Americans were fighting were "deceitful," "absolutely hostile to the white race," and unworthy of respect. The US forces even developed a new term called "protective retribution" to justify things like the slaughter on Samar.

US soldiers in Manilla during the Philippine-American War. The gun is a 3.2-inch gun M1897. Image Credit: US Library of Congress.

As the war progressed, the atrocities increased. The US Senate held hearings on the Philippine-American War between January and June in 1902. Corporal Richard O'Brien, who had fought in the Philippines, provided harrowing testimony under oath about the horrors he had witnessed, including taking orders to kill everyone in sight. O'Brien testified that he had watched the first sergeant of his company gun down a small boy and a large crowd of unarmed villagers. He also talked about two older Filipinos who came out to surrender holding a white flag and who were mowed down on the spot by American troops. These troops went into the village after that and shot everyone they could find, including a sick old man in the doorway of his home who they obliterated with "dum-dum" bullets. Dum-dum bullets are made to expand when they hit a target and leave a large exit wound, essentially exploding a huge hole in the person or thing which they hit.

In perhaps his most disturbing testimony, O'Brien spoke about a young mother begging for mercy in a village with a baby suckling at her breast as her house burned. She didn't want to leave her house because she was sure the Americans would kill her, so she stood there and burned to death with her children because, as O'Brien observed, "she feared the American soldiers, however, worse than the devouring flames."

The testimony of Corporal Daniel J. Evans before the Senate in April 1902 provided horrifying details of the torture used on the Filipinos, including a practice similar to modern-day waterboarding where several gallons of water were poured into a prisoners' mouth until they couldn't breathe. They were then tied to a post and beaten in the stomach repeatedly and quickly until the prisoner collapsed or was willing to speak. These practices were claimed as necessary to gain intelligence and save lives. Filipinos who had the "water cure" done on them sometimes died. In one recorded case, a Filipino priest, Father Augustine, was killed by US troops due to this water torture.

1902 Life magazine cartoon application of the water cure by United States Army soldiers on a Filipino. In the background, soldiers representing various European nations look on smiling. The Europeans say, "Those pious Yankees can't throw stones at us any more," i.e., can't judge us for our misdeeds anymore. Image Credit: Public Domain.

The Filipino fighters also had a seething hatred of American soldiers and committed numerous atrocities against them as well. In an 1899 report from an unnamed Filipino soldier back to Aguinaldo listing troop behavior, various indignities are recorded, including Filipino soldiers cutting off American soldiers' noses and ears, burying American prisoners of war alive, and severely beating and humiliating American prisoners during interrogations.

However, the atrocities were more plentiful on the American side of the conflict. Theodore Conley of the Kansas Regiment spoke of being ashamed of the war and of its ugly contradiction of the ideals America was founded on. In Conley's opinion, the Filipinos "are fighting as the Cubans fought against Spanish tyranny and misrule." Conley despaired, writing that the war was "reversing history" and making the American people and government "in the position occupied by Great Britain in 1776." Further, Conley denounced the war as "utterly causeless and defenseless" and "a crime against human liberty as well as against Christianity and civilization."

Corporal Robert D. Maxwell of the 20th Kansas Regiment said that the order to shoot prisoners came from pragmatism because sometimes Filipino fighters "would fall as though dead and, after we had passed, would climb a tree and shoot every soldier that passed that way." As a result, orders came down "to take no prisoners, but to shoot all."

Clarence Clowe, who had served as a private in the 25th Infantry during the war, wrote in a 1901 letter to Senator George Frisbee Hoar about his belief in the need for enhanced methods in order to win the war, writing that orders to tie up, beat, and torture prisoners despite their families crying for mercy were all accepted parts of war in order to obtain information. He also wrote that "the majority of soldiers take a keen delight" in doing such things to win the war.

Brigadier General Frederick Funston, a veteran who saw major combat action in the war and earned the Medal of Honor, had a very different perspective from horrified veterans like O'Brien, Conley, and Evans, whose conscience had been shocked by the American actions in the Philippines. Having led a successful operation to capture Aguinaldo that had been a turning point of the Philippine-American War, Funston was straightforwardly proud of his and his fellow soldiers' efforts in the Philippines and scoffed at the idea that the atrocities were of serious concern. Touring the United States in 1902 before the war's end to drum up support, Funston decried anti-war Americans and dissenters who wanted an end to the war as naïve idiots and traitors who should have been supporting the troops, saying that the perception that the Filipinos were just "fighting for the right to self-government" was foolish. They were, in his mind, "an illiterate, semi-savage people who are waging war, not against tyranny, but against Anglo-Saxon order and decency." Funston bragged about having "personally strung up thirty-five Filipinos without trial" and mocked those concerned about such actions, stating that "If more [people did this], the war would have been over long ago." Americans who wanted to pressure Congress into a peace deal were not just wrong, according to Funston; they should be executed. "For starters, all Americans who had recently petitioned Congress to sue for peace in the Philippines should be dragged out of their homes and lynched," Funston exclaimed.

The most notable massacres occurred at Lonoy on the island of Bohol in March 1901 and Balangiga on Samar Island in September 1901. In Lonoy, American soldiers killed over 400 natives, including many civilians, while in Balangiga, the Americans were caught off guard and had almost their whole garrison killed by Filipino guerilla fighters and sympathizers in the town.

Chapter 10 – The Capture of Aguinaldo

American forces had been trying to capture Aguinaldo for years, and by 1900, they were very close. In October of 1899, American scouts intercepted communications from the Filipino leader announcing that he was changing the capital to Bayombong. American troops who had been engaged in the Second San Isidro Campaign and the San Fabian Campaign rerouted to try to capture Aguinaldo. However, he always seemed to be one step ahead.

At a meeting of his council the next month, Aguinaldo said an all-out guerilla war was the answer to defeating the Americans. He took a train northward and attempted to march for Pozzorrubio in the Pangasinan province farther east. Brigadier General Gregorio del Pilar and his troops met Aguinaldo partway on the trek, growing their party size to 1,200. They arrived in Pozzorrubio on November 14. However, Aguinaldo and his men had been attacked by a strong American force along the way, and Aguinaldo's mother and son had been taken as prisoners. When the Americans reached Pozzorrubio to grab him as well, he was already gone, as he had run away over the mountains into the La Union province.

American troops under Major General Wheaton would have been in the correct place to prevent Aguinaldo's escape, having sailed from Manila on November 6 and arriving by November 7 in Fabian. Just after landing, however, Wheaton's troops were struck by a massive storm that flooded everything and completely stopped their ability to march into position. This delayed them by almost a week, and Wheaton's troops couldn't reach Pozzorrubio until November 16, by which time Aguinaldo had already escaped.

Major General Lawton had wished to send Brigadier General Samuel Young northward to seize Aguinaldo, but General Elwell Otis said that instead, the soldiers should guard any access to the east. Young went east with 1,100 men, heading for Tayug, Pangasinan, in order to block any attempt by Aguinaldo to get away again.

Reaching Naguilian in the La Union province by November 17, Aguinaldo was outwitted by Brigadier General Young, who suspected that Aguinaldo might turn east toward Candon and had sent a battalion to stop his advance. The battalion, commanded by Major Peyton Marsh, engaged Aguinaldo's defensive troops at the Battle of Tirad Pass, with General Gregorio del Pilar dying in the fight. The Filipinos, numbering only just over 60, sacrificed their lives in a suicide mission to delay the more than 500 American troops from advancing to get Aguinaldo. Aguinaldo, for his part, had gotten away again. He had been set up with a small group of soldiers around ten kilometers (a little over six miles) south of Tirad Pass, and when a messenger came to tell him about the bloodbath going on nearby, he left for the Cayan settlement with his men.

The American attempt to get Aguinaldo was proving to be very difficult indeed. His top generals and key revolutionary leaders began to fall, with Martin Delgado surrendering on January 10 at Panay. Delgado had become a hero after leading resistance against the Americans conquering Panay, although he would later be elected the governor of Panay under American approval from 1902 to 1904 and later serve as the head of a leprosy-curing sanitorium in Santa Barbara.

General Frederick Funston led the troops who ultimately captured Aguinaldo, coming across him on March 23, 1901, in the small village of Palanan in the Isabela province. The Americans were aided by the Philippine Scouts, whose ranks were filled with Filipinos who had come over to the American side to fight and who detested their longtime enemies, the Tagalog—of whom Aguinaldo was the ultimate head. Play-acting that they had been taken captive by the scouts, who were donned in Filipino army uniforms, American troops gained access to Aguinaldo's home base, and then they and the Philippine Scouts attacked his guards and seized the Filipino leader. They finally had Aguinaldo.

The capture of their leader was a big blow to the Filipino forces, with revolutionary leader Nicolas Capistrano surrendering on March 29 and troops beginning to wane in terms of their morale. Emilio Aguinaldo formally accepted American authority in the Philippines on April 1, 1901, at Malacañan Palace in Manila and signed a formal surrender letter on April 19. At this time, Aguinaldo formally proceeded with the end of the official hostilities, and he ordered his troops to put their weapons and stop fighting. According to Aguinaldo, he had, as the proclamation read, decided that "the complete termination of hostilities and a lasting peace are not only desirable but also absolutely essential for the well-being of the Philippines."

The surrenders began to roll in after Aguinaldo's capture, with Manuel Tinio and José Alejandrino surrendering on April 29, Mariano Trías surrendering in the south of Luzon on May 13, and Major General Pantaleon Garcia, commander of Central Luzon, giving up in May. Generals Servillano Aquino, Francisco Macabulos, Juan Cailles, and Pío del Pilar surrendered in June, with revolutionary leader Vito Belarmino also doing so on July 4. Aguinaldo remained on the run for almost a year until September 1901, when he set up a new base at Palanan.

President McKinley's time as the leader of the United States was also drawing to a close but not due to his term as president ending. The day after speaking in September of 1901 at the Pan-Am Exposition in Buffalo, New York, and extolling the virtues of America's new global duties to bring civilization and order, McKinley was gunned down at a public gathering by a Polish anarchist named Leon Czolgosz. The shocked crowd screamed as McKinley fell to the ground, a bullet lodged in his stomach. He was bleeding profusely and died exactly eight days after the shooting. War hero Theodore Roosevelt stepped into the picture at this point, ready to take the reins and go all out in the Philippines.

Around a week later, the aforementioned Balangiga ambush occurred. Forty-eight American troops got up to eat in the morning, and instead of enjoying breakfast, they were slashed and killed in a surprise attack by Filipinos. The Balangiga massacre, around 400 miles to the southeast of Manila on the island of Samar, was horrifying to the American public, for whom it drove home the horrors of the war. The 24 surviving American soldiers told terrifying stories of the Filipinos hacking them limb from limb and depicted the attack as a dishonorable slaughter against the rules of war. This attack was what led to General Jacob Smith ordering to kill any Filipino over ten years of age who was physically able to fight the Americans. The order eventually led to the court-martial of Smith and three other officers as a token gesture of reprisal from the largely approving Roosevelt, with none of the men receiving any serious punishment for their actions.

The fighting continued after Aguinaldo's surrender and well into 1901. The Filipino independence fighters were now led by several Filipino leaders in Batangas and Samar—Miguel Malvar and Vincente Lukbán, respectively. Technically, Malvar became the new leader of the First Philippine Republic after Aguinaldo, consolidating the thousands of under armed troops at his command into the so-called "Army of Liberation" and assembling them in southern Luzon. Lukbán was taken as a prisoner of war in February

of 1902, and Malvar was seized by US forces on April 16, 1902, bringing their resistance attempts to a close.

Chapter 11 – Filipinos Are Defeated

As hard as the Filipinos had fought, the war was only going in one direction: American victory. Since Aguinaldo was now captured and more and more Filipinos were not interested in resisting American administration, the dream of independence slowly faded. Although to be fair, much of the American zest for impressing their norms on the Filipinos and administrating the islands, no matter the cost, had also dissolved in its intensity.

The Americans had better—and much more—guns than the Filipinos from the very beginning. In fact, historians estimate the Filipinos had only 20,000 rifles for their entire army by the middle of 1901 and often had only one gun for three soldiers. The Americans were not hesitant to use their weaponry to devastating effect, with Rear Admiral George Dewey, for example, motoring down the Pasig River and incinerating Filipino positions at point-blank range with half-ton shells in what US troops laughed about as "quail" hunting. During many battles of the war, the Americans killed so many Filipinos that the Americans sometimes piled up corpses to provide defensive cover.

Throughout the war, the Filipinos had more soldiers but not enough guns and weapons for them. Some even used handmade spears and homemade weapons like darts to try to take on the Americans, while others grabbed guns from dead compatriots. They did have some modern rifles that they had snuck in from foreign countries or taken from the Spanish, but overall, the Filipinos often had lousy old guns that could barely aim and were sorely lacking in effective firepower against the avalanche of American lead. It was very hard for the Filipinos to get in more weapons throughout the war, as the Americans had moved quickly right at the beginning to cut off water access and enforce a naval blockade.

Although Filipino fighters used any edge they could find, such as the terrain and the climate, they had bled and died in large numbers throughout the war and watched as their hometowns and families were burned to the ground by the Americans in response. General Elwell Otis may have been optimistic at the beginning that the war would soon be over, but he was soon proven wrong by the need for more US troops in the continuing insurgency. However, even with this in mind, it was still clear that Aguinaldo and his men simply did not stand a chance, especially once Major General MacArthur came in with a more hard-headed approach, remarking that it would take a decade of "bayonet treatment" to subdue the Filipinos and that he was willing to be the one to administer the treatment if necessary. As MacArthur saw it, fear alone had not been enough to win the war and what was needed was for defectors and traitors to come over to the American side as well, something that steadily began to happen.

By November of 1899 and the re-election of McKinley, the Filipino guerrilla effort had major issues, having hoped that their fierce resistance would lead to McKinley losing the confidence of the American public. The truth was the public was not paying very much attention to the war. Even as mass atrocities were alleged, such as the murder of 1,000 Filipino prisoners of war at Sorsogon, the public remained largely unconvinced and unengaged, particularly as the US Department of War denied the reports and said there was no proof.

With the capture of Aguinaldo, the war began to close down. When Malvar surrendered, it became clear that the war was rapidly winding to a close. However, not all of Malvar's men surrendered; so, of course, the fighting continued, and new leaders of the independence struggle still emerged after the war to continue the fight, even in places the Americans thought had already been conquered.

The war had become one giant, overwhelming headache, with hundreds of thousands dead and not much will to keep it going on either side, although the United States was certainly committed to pouring in more reinforcements and armaments if necessary to ensure a victory, despite the casualties and costs. With President Theodore Roosevelt now at the helm—a former champion of democracy-building at gunpoint—one would think enthusiasm would be at an all-time high, but even Roosevelt conceded that imperialism and empire-building was not something the United States was well suited for or should have an abiding commitment to going forward.

Chapter 12 – Guerilla Fighting Continues after the Official End of the War

US President Theodore Roosevelt officially declared victory in the conflict on July 2, 1902. Nonetheless, hostilities continued with varying degrees of intensity until 1913. Roosevelt's announcement also granted clemency to any Filipino—except Moros who were still fighting the Americans and Filipinos for independence—who had fought against the United States. From the Filipino perspective, the war ended on April 16, 1902, after the surrender of General Malvar, something which was announced by former President of the Philippines Gloria Arroyo in 2002.

Two major campaigns after the official end of the war were the Mindanao campaign from July 1902 to December 1904 and the Jolo Campaign, which occurred in the spring of 1905 and 1906 and the summer of 1913.

The Mindanao conflict first flared up in 1902 when the Muslim population on Mindanao and the Sulu islands started to go on the attack, burning villages and rising up against the occupying

Americans. Colonel Frank Baldwin was dispatched to crush the Moro with an infantry company and a mountain battery about 1,000 strong. Baldwin defeated the forces of the Sultan of Bayan on May 2, 1902, near Lake Lanao, while Captain John Pershing famously headed an expedition in 1903 that gave rise to all sorts of false urban legends—including one repeated several times on the campaign trail by US President Donald Trump—about dipping bullets in pig's blood and shooting the Muslim fighters with them to desecrate their bodies and break the morale of the nearby fighters. Another force led by Captain Frank McCoy eventually succeeded in gunning down Moro leader Dato Ali in October 1905.

By October of 1902, the fighting was intense in Albay when a force led by rebel leader Simeón Ola would not listen to American demands to put down their weapons. Around 20,000 American troops were still on the islands, but Filipino troops were sent to put down the uprising. Laws were passed to make it a crime punishable by death to resist American rule by participating in a guerrilla group, although, obviously, this had already been taking place; the law just made it official. By the time Ola gave up to US troops in 1903, the fighting was still ongoing, and over 300,000 Filipinos had been imprisoned in concentration camps.

Combat continued on Cavite where a revolutionary society had been founded once more by one of Aguinaldo's top men, General Luciano San Miguel, who had distinguished himself throughout the Philippine-American War with his brave exploits and fierce fighting even in hopeless circumstances. Over 350 battles took place just in 1903 alone, after the war was officially over, to give a sense of the scale of the continued hostilities. Taft and Roosevelt were mortified and furious, and troops began adopting more targeted anti-insurgency tactics, such as taking a census, instituting identification cards, and making it clear that any villagers who supplied rebels would be severely punished, although this did not work very well. Another member of Aguinaldo's government, General Artemio Ricarte, who had been captured early in the war, is a good example of the incompetence of the post-war American efforts to stomp out the insurgency.

American troops gave Ricarte the option of switching sides to ally with the United States early in the war when he was captured, but he would not do it. He was summarily deported to Guam and then came back to Manila; however, he would still not join the US and was therefore deported again, this time to Hong Kong. Ricarte was enraged by the constant deportations and threats and started talking more and more to other independence fighters and figures, sneaking back into the Philippines at the end of 1903. Now back in his homeland, Ricarte coordinated with other guerrillas, helping train further resistance activities and supplying and organizing troops. It took many more months for the Americans to capture him again, humiliating them for their lack of ability to quickly seize and incapacitate him and his troops.

More fighting erupted on Samar by the summer of 1904, and an American-installed mayor was burned alive, with a gasoline-soaked American flag wrapped around his head as a warning to others loyal to the flag, according to rebel leader Juliano Caducoy. American soldiers faced fierce resistance and were set upon frequently by determined Filipino fighters, who stole their weapons and routed them. The fighting continued for two years, and American troops had to be reinforced several times on Samar before the resistance was finally crushed in 1905.

Battles continued erupting in other locations in Rizal, Laguna, and Malabon through 1904 and 1905. Many ordinary Filipinos still sympathized with the independence fighters, particularly the lower working class who had been left out of the benefits the *Ilustrados* enjoyed, leading to attacks on authority figures, banks, and other institutions. The rebels did not fight openly anymore, instead blending seamlessly in and out of the civilian population in order to inflict maximum damage.

As the fighting continued, it became clear that the war would not be easily wrapped up and concluded. In mid-Luzon, combat still continued in places, and the pursuit of the rebel leader Macario Sakay was still ongoing. While Aguinaldo had ultimately given up his ambitions and was relaxing on a large 500-hectare estate in Cavite, others like Sakay, who were not a part of the *Ilustrados*, were still fighting hard. While Aguinaldo and other former leaders concurred with the official American position that people like Sakay were nothing but worthless *ladrones* (bandits), those who had fought against the Americans during the war saw their actions as a natural continuation of the struggle for independence and self-determination. Sakay was seen by some as the one who could successfully take up the banner for independence after Aguinaldo, so capturing him was an American priority.

By 1906, the Americans managed to capture Sakay, as well as Julian Montalan and Lucio de Vega, other important rebel leaders. Any chance of effective resistance to American rule was basically over, but the fighting still went on in Mindanao, where Muslim Filipinos were outraged at the attempt to override their Islamic way of life. Largely separate from the questions and struggles of the Philippine-American War, they were disgusted at having the American victory over the northern fighters seen as a victory over them as well. As previously mentioned, the Philippines was not really a unified "nation" in the sense Westerners may conceive the term. The Moros did not consider themselves allied with the Tagalog or the Filipinos who wanted independence; they wanted it for themselves and for their own tribal and religious reasons. The Mindanao resistance was usually done by entire communities, and the Americans responded by killing everyone in said community—slaughtering more than 600 men, women, and children in Mount Dajo in March of 1906, for example. The fighting in Mindanao—which was in the news in recent years because of ISIS militants fighting against the Filipino government there—continued all the way until 1916.

Fighting broke out again on the island of Negros, which had formerly been mostly pro-American and "pacified." The fighting was led by rebel leader Dionisio Magbuelas, more commonly known as Papa Isio, a farmer-turned-fighter who had led various rebel groups in the hills of the island. Most of his fighters came from sugar cane workers (*sacadas*) who were underpaid and sick of being exploited. They had been further radicalized after America's entrance into the war and watched as their former bosses joined the American side. By the time of the post-war fighting, Papa Isio was an urban legend and a hero around the Philippines, and he had succeeded in taking over the village of Isabela. He was not captured until August 1907. He was charged with banditry and crimes against the Americans and was sentenced to death; however, his sentence was changed to life in prison, and he died in Bilibid Prison in 1911.

By this point, the main group left fighting was led by Felipe Salvador. His organization, the "Santa Iglesia," had started prior to the Philippine-American War, and he became a colonel in Aguinaldo's army. He refused to lay down arms when the war ended and broke out of jail after he was captured by the Americans. Salvador continued to cause trouble for the Americans around Luzon, including attacking the police in a major attack at Malolos. Putting down Salvador's rebellion became a priority for the United States, especially as he was not only advocating independence but also pushing a number of anti-capitalist positions, including breaking up the wealthy land-owning monopolies and redistributing the lands to the working class. Salvador was not captured until 1912 when he was convicted of "banditry" and executed.

The biggest battle of the Mindanao Campaign and the fight against the Moro people was on December 12, 1904, at the Battle of Dolores River, where 43 Constabulary Scouts under the command of American Lieutenant Stephen Hayt were hit by a surprise attack by over 1,000 Pulahan fighters. Fighting desperately for their lives, the scouts managed to inflict heavy casualties on the advancing fighters, killing around 300, but they could not ultimately hold them off.

Thirty-seven scouts were killed in action during the fierce fighting along the Dolores River.

The Jolo Campaign in 1905, 1906, and 1913 was another major bout of conflict after the official end of the Philippine-American War. American forces and Filipino scouts had to fight various rebel factions from the Moro on the island of Jolo in 1905. The fierce fighting eventually resulted in surrender, while in 1906, the First Battle of Bud Dajo led to an American victory. The First Battle of Bud Dajo, which lasted from March 5 to 7, 1906, was quite unique, as it occurred when a contingent of over 1,000 Moro people went inside a volcano crater and attacked Americans from inside it before almost all being killed, including women and children. The Second Battle of Bud Dajo occurred in December of 1911 and lasted five days.

Three Moros rebels hung in Jolo on July 23, 1911. Image Credit: Wikimedia, Public Domain

It erupted after 1,500 Moros rebuilt defenses in the dormant volcano and began fighting American forces. General Pershing managed to talk most of them out, but those who stayed in, loyal to a leader of theirs called Jailani, were almost all killed. Lastly, there was fighting in the summer of 1913 at Bagsac, where the Moros were again brutally defeated.

Conclusion: The Philippine-America War: Lessons (Un)learned

Due to the harsh entanglement of the Philippine-American War, the US government was hesitant for decades about getting involved in global military engagements. Although the First and Second World Wars would once again bring America into the global theater of war, the Philippine-American War was a major blow to the imperial ambitions of the United States.

After the Japanese invaded the Philippines during the Second World War, General Arthur MacArthur's son, Douglas MacArthur, became a hero for helping drive the Japanese out of the Philippines at the cost of over 60,000 dead American soldiers and one million dead Filipinos. On July 4, 1946—America's Independence Day—the Philippines was granted full independence by the United States.

The war with the Philippines would come to be enveloped in a kind of fog and a deluge of propaganda that downplayed its tragedies and played up the atmosphere of Manifest Destiny and American righteousness. As the *realpolitik* of America's economic and military competition with Spain collided with its high-minded rhetoric about self-determination and democracy, the Philippine-American War was a stain on the national conscience. Although egged on by a supportive mass media, the business community, and a cadre of imperialist politicians from the post-Civil War Republican Party, the venture into the Philippines showed how badly one could get burned if one does not watch what one is doing and why.

Anti-imperialists, like William Jennings Bryan, Andrew Carnegie, and former President Grover Cleveland, were not on board with the war and joined the Anti-Imperialist League to make a stand. Generally speaking, the American public had not been told about the reason of why some Filipinos were fighting and instead were guided by editorials and commentaries about how the natives needed a strong hand in order to grow up and learn to govern themselves. Journalists who were covering the war were often restricted in terms of what details and information they could include in their reports, and as mentioned previously, censorship was put in place once the war became less public relations-friendly. The few members of the press who were on the scene, government announcements, and military news were the only ways the American public could find out what was going on. Invariably, of course, official sources painted a rosy picture, and reporters who didn't toe the line were soon given a one-way ticket home.

Coverage of Aguinaldo's original Declaration of Independence was run in one US paper (the *San Francisco Chronicle*) and was given a headline of "Aguinaldo Plans to Become Dictator." The newspapers and official reports were full of bravado about how noble the US mission was, also obscuring the real start of the war and saying that the Filipinos had fired first along with numerous other lies. The enormous casualties on the Filipino side were justified by the media as well; for instance, an 1899 *Chicago Times-Herald* editorial argued that "only by a crushing repulse of the Filipinos could our position be made secure" and that as the guarantor of "civilization and peace" America was compelled to act.

US military leaders were true believers in the backwardness and irrelevance of what they termed the "Philippine Insurrection," with Military Governor-General Elwell Otis, for example, characterizing Aguinaldo as a worthless "tribal chieftain" who needed to be snuffed out as quickly as possible and not taken seriously as a voice in the conversation about the future of the islands. Otis put out a press release each day, hyping victories and always presenting them as the final push to a great and glorious victory. He also detailed and embellished the horrors inflicted on the Americans by the Filipinos in order to bolster support at home and among the troops.

The information war was—and still is—king. General Joseph Wheeler, also a master at the art of war propaganda, helped provide stories of horrors as well, calling the independence fighters "Aguinaldo's Dusky Demons" and claiming they were staging their own atrocities and murdering their own women and children in order to blame innocent American soldiers.

Otis, believing his own propaganda about how the war was almost over and how the final victory was approaching, was slow to accept the need for reinforcements. It was partly for this reason that he was relieved of command by McKinley in April of 1900. He was replaced by General Arthur MacArthur, who admitted the need for reinforcements and adopted a more realistic position.

While the Americans may have needed more reinforcements for the war, their losses in the war were nowhere near what they inflicted on the Filipino soldiers. By the end of 1902, there had been almost 20,000 Filipino fighters killed in action and 4,230 American soldiers killed in action, not to mention the estimated 250,000 to one million Filipino civilians who lost their lives due to side-effects of the war (such as famine or disease) or directly because of it. Statistics showed vastly more Filipino soldiers were killed in action rather than being taken as prisoners of war, something that the American military leadership said was because they were just better shots.

As in Vietnam, stories of atrocities, torture, and murder of civilians began to emerge—slowly and cautiously, since US-based editors had a hard time finding proof. In time, letters from soldiers, which were not censored, began to tell a very different tale from the rollicking exploits detailed by Otis and Wheeler. Occasional stories about American actions began to make it into the media but were vastly outweighed by the stories of the horrors and savagery of the Filipino enemy and their irrational resistance to American benevolence. General Jacob Smith's October 1901 order on the island of Samar to shoot and kill anyone over ten eventually did cause a stir in the United States, but it was quickly defused by President Roosevelt, who ordered a court-martial on Smith but basically did almost nothing to punish him except slapping Smith on the wrist in the form of an early retirement. As Roosevelt put it, Smith's unfortunate orders were understandable given due to the "cruel and barbarous savages" the Americans were fighting in the Philippines.

President Richard Nixon pursued a similar and effective strategy in response to the My Lai Massacre in March 1968, where US troops killed between 347 to 504 defenseless South Vietnamese civilians—including babies, children, and women—engaged in violent gang rapes of women, and butchered fleeing civilians in broad daylight. My Lai led to the 1971 conviction of the leader of the platoon which was responsible for this massacre, US Army Second Lieutenant William Calley, Jr. Twenty-six soldiers were charged for crimes from the massacre, but only Calley was convicted. At his trial, Calley said he was just doing the same as "any good soldier would do," and the ruling Judge James Robert Elliott sympathized, stating "war is war, and it's not unusual for innocent civilians such as the My Lai victims to be killed." Calley, who was originally given a life sentence, ultimately served only three and a half years of house arrest for his role in killing 22 civilians during the massacre. Calley's defense that he was just doing his job was a very similar defense to that used by many Nazi war criminals during the Nuremberg trials and by members of the Bush administration in the aftermath of the

Abu Ghraib situation, where Iraqis were being tortured and raped by US personnel.

When US Secretary of War Elihu Root spoke in 1902, he expressed the prevailing outlook of the time on the Philippine-American War, namely that the conflict had overall been fought with the most respect possible for the Filipinos and with a "scrupulous regard for the rules of civilized warfare," as well as "genuine consideration for the prisoner and the non-combatant." According to Root—and the media and military establishment—the war had been marked by "self-restraint" and an unparalleled degree of "humanity." At the height of the war, it's worth mentioning that Root had endorsed the necessity for the "tough methods" American forces used because they had "proved successful" against hostile Native American tribes in the United States.

Nonetheless, the reports of Brigadier General Franklin Bell's concentration camps reached home and shocked the public, leading to a Senate inquiry pushed by anti-imperialist politicians. It fell flat since the Republican majority made sure it never came out from behind closed doors. The press admitted some complicity and expressed sorrow at the camps, but overall, the issue began to depress people, and it faded from their minds because of its unpleasantness. This "reconcentration" tactic, as it was called, was carried out in the Batangas and Laguna provinces in order to basically strip the Filipino independence movement of any covert or overt civilian infrastructure or support. Bell said it was also being done to "protect" the villagers from the Filipino fighters. Villagers were allowed to bring their animals and as much food as they could carry with them, and by January 1902, the Americans began razing all the crops, humans, and livestock outside the concentration camp areas to the ground in what Bell termed a "pacification" mission. Bell also told his units not to record the missions or the collateral damage, as about seventeen percent of Luzon's entire population died in the camps and from ensuing starvation.

It is impossible at this point for historians to know exactly how many civilians died from disease and starvation as opposed to being casualties of war, although most reputable historians of the Philippine-American War agree that the vast majority died from disease and starvation. The use of concentration camps—which had been used by the British against the Dutch in South Africa in 1900 to 1902 and by Spain against the Cubans in the Spanish-Cuban War of 1895 to 1898—were employed in order to basically force the surrounding combat environment into a black and white scenario, with the civilians all in one area and the combatants everywhere else. The Spanish, under General Valeriano Weyler ("the Butcher"), had contributed to the deaths of hundreds of thousands of Cubans in their camps during the Spanish-Cuban War, which was part of what had horrified the American public and spurred them to strongly support the American war against Spain in 1898 to free Cuba from Spanish rule. Unlike the concentration camps infamously used by the Third Reich during the Second World War, the primary purpose of the concentration camps used by Spain, Britain, America, and other colonial powers at this time was not to kill those interned inside but to hold them while the army destroyed any combatants outside; they were basically poorly managed and disease-ridden holding zones. Although murder was not the tactical goal, tens of thousands of civilians perished in the harsh conditions of the hastily erected camps from lack of proper food and the dirty conditions that led to massive cholera outbreaks.

As the Americans battled a relatively tiny number of guerillas across a nation of millions, they essentially wanted to separate out combatants from non-combatants. They were exceedingly frustrated by the lack of clarity in determining who exactly was fighting them and who was just an innocent civilian, particularly as many Filipinos in Aguinaldo's forces would blend in and do civilian jobs during the day and then go on the attack at night, hunting down American forces. The concentration camps and concentration zones were the unfortunate outcomes of America's frustration.

A major problem for the Americans resulted from their inability to penetrate the guerrilla infrastructure. They soon began to realize, to their dismay, that a whole underground network loyal to the guerrillas existed, even in areas considered thoroughly "pacified." When a town was occupied, the stars and stripes flew, and gratifying expressions of loyalty and support for the American cause were publicly proclaimed by town officials. But reliable information about the guerrillas was almost never forthcoming, supplies and equipment were forever disappearing, and occasionally, an American soldier would stray too far from camp and be found the next day hacked to pieces by a bolo knife, which is similar to a machete. Albert Robinson, one of a handful of American newsmen covering the war (and the most ingenious when it came to getting around General Elwell Otis' strict censorship), wrote that unqualified US control in the Philippines extended "about as far as a Krag-Jorgensen [the main type of rifle used by the Americans during the war] could throw a bullet."

By early 1900, US outposts were being established everywhere. As a rule, the Filipinos allowed the Americans to capture and occupy any town they wished without opposition. Elwell Otis was so deceived by this that he once again declared flatly that the war was over, hoping perhaps that the repetition of that statement would make it so. But the garrison network seriously thinned the US troops' strength, and the Americans were continually being counterattacked and ambushed. It was becoming clear that the entire islands would have to be "pacified." Moreover, guerrilla activity was both increasing and becoming increasingly effective. Being incessantly ambushed, boloed, and betrayed was nerve-wracking, and the Americans began to exercise their mounting frustration on the population at large. All the Filipinos were enemies in their eyes, whether or not they bore arms. Patrols sent to fight the guerrillas usually had difficulty locating the enemy and often resorted to burning local neighborhoods in their path. Village officials were often forced at bayonet point to lead American patrols, and non-combatants began to be held responsible for the actions of the guerrillas. Any form of resistance to American objectives subjected the perpetrator to a charge of treason.

Press censorship was so effective that few Americans actually knew the difficulties being experienced in the Philippines, or, in fact, that there were 70,000 US troops on the islands. In early 1900, the first whiff of a scandal reached American shores when it was disclosed that the American forces had been issued "dum-dum" bullets, which was a breach of the 1899 Hague Convention concerning humane warfare (which the US had conveniently neglected to ratify). Reports of the burning of villages, the killing of non-combatants, and the application of the "water cure" to elicit information began to filter back to the US. Often this information was contained in letters written by US soldiers to their families which found their way into local newspapers. A typical example from an unnamed soldier in the 43rd Infantry: "On Thursday, March 29th …eighteen of my company killed seventy-five nigger bolomen and ten of the nigger gunners…When we find one who is not dead, we have bayonets…"

In addition to concentration camps and concentration zones, the United States tried to weed out guerillas by taking away supplies, deporting uncooperative citizens from their military government-controlled districts, burning crops, and killing those who would not give them information or appeared to be hostile on sight in public executions.

Philippine Insurrection, 1899-1902. Burning of the native district in Manila called Tondo, undated. Image Credit: US Library of Congress.

Originally referred to as the Philippine Insurrection as part of the American campaign to write and glorify its own history, the war was officially re-designated as the Philippine-American War in 1999 by the US Library of Congress.

Even those who retain a more positive view of America's involvement in the Philippines during the war would have to acknowledge that the United States got in over its head in the islands and did not really have a solid plan. On such a multipolar battlefield, the realities and combatants were shifting day by day, and the idea of treating the conflict as black and white or easily justifiable is just not feasible.

However, it is true that with their victory, the power and global reach of the United States expanded immensely, and it now had the Asian foothold it so desired. The Philippines gave America enormous naval, military, economic, and geostrategic powers, and in that sense, it was a success for American interests. Although many modern historians recognize the horrors and atrocities of the war, some such as Eric Love do maintain that overall it was better than what could have happened if another colonial power such as Japan, Germany, Britain, or Russia had come into the Philippines instead. Worse still, if multiple colonial powers faced off against the Filipinos, each with a fanatical desperation to achieve victory, they could have potentially enacted an even more brutal and scorched-earth campaign than the Americans did.

Nowadays, however, with America's ongoing close relationship with the Philippines in a desire to offset Chinese power, the bitter fighting of the Philippine-American War has been safely buried in the past. Through the course of nine American presidents, the Philippines struggled and muddled its way to independence. Although it started with McKinley, which began with their annexation in 1899 until his assassination in 1901, the reins were soon taken over by Theodore Roosevelt, who oversaw the presidency from the middle of the war until he left his post in 1909. Taft followed after until Woodrow Wilson took over in 1913, with Warren Harding (1921–1923), Calvin Coolidge (1923–1929), Herbert Hoover (1929–1933), and Franklin Delano Roosevelt (1933–1945) filling the role of president. Harry Truman was the last president who oversaw the struggle of the Filipinos trying to gain their independence, which was granted in 1946 following the Second World War. Their independence was a very specific agreement between the United States and the Philippines that can credibly be argued to have basically maintained the American economic and social dominance inherent in the Spanish- and American-made governmental and municipal systems constructed during colonialism, which still exists in various forms—economically, class-wise, racially, and socially—in the Philippines to this day.

Speaking before the Philippine Congress in October 2003, US President George W. Bush presented a perfect encapsulation of the sanitized, mythologized version of Philippine-American relations, saying that "together our soldiers liberated the Philippines from colonial rule." That's certainly one way to put it—if you leave out the other half of the story. Although American and Filipino history includes fights against both the Spanish colonizers and the Japanese imperialists in the Second World War, the conflict of 1899–1902 is important to never forget for those who are interested in the complexity of real history, diplomatic relations and geopolitical struggle rather than the feel-good rhetoric of politicians or briefly summarized generalizations. Yes, the United States and the Philippines have been close—even indispensable—friends, but they have also been the bitterest of enemies.

In many ways, the Philippine-American War continues to be the background to today's debates about the role of America on the global stage. It was the spark that lit the powder keg of America's global ambitions and turned it into a colony-holding superpower. The issues at the heart of the Philippine-American War are still very much relevant in American conflicts ongoing in the Middle East, Africa, and South Asia. For better or for worse, for sincere reasons or for false, how much responsibility or motivation should the American government have for intervening in the affairs, problems, and struggles of foreign nations? This is a question that is not going to go away any time soon.

It is the hope of the author that this book has provided a fair hearing to the different perspectives on the Philippine-American War and that it helped readers gain insights and information on the high costs of the conflict which reshaped the Philippines and was America's first major appearance on the world stage in terms of overseas empire-building.

Check out more books by Captivating History

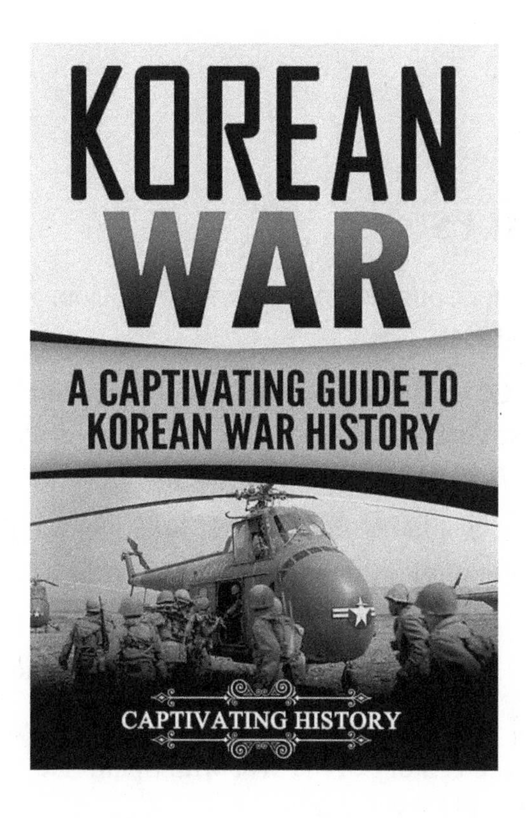
KOREAN
WAR
A CAPTIVATING GUIDE TO
KOREAN WAR HISTORY
CAPTIVATING HISTORY

References:

Albert Beveridge, Congressional Record, 56th Congress, 1st sess., 1900, 33: 704–12.

As Our Might Grows Less: The Philippine-American War in Context by Jose Angeles (Approved dissertation for Ph. D. at the University of Oregon) https://core.ac.uk/download/pdf/36692260.pdf

1898: Our Last Men in the Philippines (2016 Spanish film showing the Spanish point of view about their conflict with the Filipinos from 1896-1898).

Heneral Luna (2015 Filipino film showing the Filipino point of view of the Philippine-American War)

Harper's Pictorial History of the War with Spain (New York: Harper and bros, 1899), 434.Available: http://www.loc.gov/rr/hispanic/1898/hay.html

Ablett, Phillip. Colonialism in Denial: US Propaganda in the Philippine-American War

https://www.researchgate.net/publication/260125750_Colonialism_in_Denial_US_Propaganda_in_the_Philippine-American_War

Linn, Brian McAllister (2000). *The Philippine War, 1899-1902.* University Press of Kansas.

Craig, James (Maj.). Federal Volunteer Regiment in the Philippine Insurrection: The History of the 32nd Infantry (United States Volunteers), 1899 to 1901.
https://apps.dtic.mil/dtic/tr/fulltext/u2/a451795.pdf

The Philippine-American War: Compassion or Conquest? By Elizabeth Holm
https://conservancy.umn.edu/bitstream/handle/11299/162537/Holm%2CElizabeth_MLS_Thesis.pdf?sequence=1&isAllowed=y

Pedro Paterno, "Proclamation of War" (June 2, 1898). Available: MSC Communications Technologies, The Philippine Centennial Celebration. http://www.msc.edu.ph/centennial/pa990602.html

David Traxel, 1898: The Birth of the American Century (New York: Alfred Knopf, 1998), p. 244.

Jose, Vicencio. *Rise and Fall of Antonio Luna*. Solar Publishing Corporation.

Silby, Dr. David J., A War of Empire and Frontier
https://www.youtube.com/watch?v=0KulM23bEIA

The Philippine-American War in 4 Minutes:
https://www.youtube.com/watch?v=scho0YzzPu8

Treaty of Paris Ratified, PBS https://www.pbs.org/crucible/tl18.html

The Filipino-American War:
https://www.youtube.com/watch?v=6y1v1Z3Zeps

The Philippine-American War, The Shocking Truth:
https://www.youtube.com/watch?v=bN2wrZGcs8s

Philippine-American War Timeline by the Philippine Study Group of Minnesota: https://www.crcworks.org/timeline.pdf

The Philippine-American War By Doug Kotlarczyk:
https://www.niu.edu/cseas/_pdf/lesson-plans/fulbright-hays/philippine-american-war.pdf

The Philippine-American War:
https://www.etownschools.org/cms/lib/PA01000774/Centricity/Domain/629/The%20Philippine%20American%20War101.pdf

Our Future in the Pacific: What We Have There to Hold and Win, The North American Review 166 (March 1898). Available: Cornell University Library, Making of America
http://cdl.library.cornell.edu/cgi-bin/moa/moa-cgi?notisid=ABQ7578-0166&byte=112663541

The Philippine-American War, By Encyclopedia Britannica Editors:
https://www.britannica.com/event/Philippine-American-War

Savage Acts: Wars, Fairs and Empire, 1898-1904 By the American Social History Project at CUNY:
https://ashp.cuny.edu/sites/default/files/savageacts-viewerguide111.pdf

The Philippine-American War, By National Center for History UCLA. https://www.learner.org/courses/amerhistory/pdf/Philippine-War_L-One.pdf

Aguinaldo, Emiliano. "Gen. Emilano Aguinaldo's Manifesto of Jan 5, 1899." 1899. TS. Web. July 19, 2019.
http://www.eastconn.org/tah/1112KM4_ACaseGuiltShameAmnesiaPhilippineAmericanlesson.pdf

Bass, John. "Dispatch." Harper's Weekly 42 (October 15, 1898), 1008. Annenberg Learner. Web. 5 Apr. 2015.
http://www.learner.org/courses/amerhistory/pdf/Philippine-War_L-One.pdf Beveridge, Albert. Congressional Record, 56th Congress, 1st sess., 1900, 33: 704-12. Annenberg Learner. Web. July 19, 2019

Captain Elliot. "Captain Elliott, of the Kansas Regiment, February 27th." Being Materials for a History of a War of Criminal Aggression. TS. George Mason University. July 19, 2019.
http://historymatters.gmu.edu/

Luther, A.J. Pictorial History of Our War with Spain for Cuba's Freedom. Freedom Publishing Company, 1898. 546. Annenberg

Learner. Web. 5 Apr. 2015.
http://www.learner.org/courses/amerhistory/pdf/Philippine-War_L-One.pdf

McKinley, William. "The Benevolent Assimilation Proclamation." 1899. TS. Eastconn.org. Web. July 19, 2019.
http://www.eastconn.org/tah/1112KM4_ACaseGuiltShameAmnesia PhilippineAmericanlesson.pdf

O'Brien, Richard. "Testimony of Corporal Richard O'Brien." 1902. TS. Eastconn.org. Web. July 19, 2019.
http://tah.eastconn.org/tah/1112KM4_ACaseGuiltShameAmnesiaPhilippineAmericanlesson.pdf

Roosevelt, Theodore, "The Strenuous Life," The Strenuous Life: Essays and Addresses (New York: Century, 1900), 115. Annenberg Learner. Web. July 19, 2019.

http://www.learner.org/courses/amerhistory/pdf/Philippine-War_L-One.pdf

Rusting, James. "Interview with President William McKinley," The Christian Advocate 22. January 1903, 17. Web. July 19, 2019.
http://historymatters.gmu.edu/d/5575/

White, Trumball. Pictorial History of Our War with Spain for Cuba's Freedom. Freedom Publishing Company, 1898. 399. Annenberg Learner. Web. July 19, 2019.
http://www.learner.org/courses/amerhistory /pdf/Philippine-War_L-One.pdf

Ablett, Phillip. "Colonialism in Denial: US Propaganda in the Philippine--American War." Social Alternatives 23.3 (2004): 22-28. Academic Search Premier. Web. July 19, 2019.

Frerichs, Luke. Foundations of Empire: The American Military Government in the Philippine-American War 1899-1902
https://scholarworks.wm.edu/cgi/viewcontent.cgi?referer=https://www.google.ca/&httpsredir=1&article=1993&context=honorstheses

Weber, Edward; Beam, Kathryn: American Involvement in the Philippines 1880-1930. https://deepblue.lib.umich.edu/bitstream/handle/2027.42/120276/American_involvement_98.pdf?sequence=1&isAllowed=y

Ellis, Elisabeth Gaynor, and Anthony Ester. World History. United States: Pearson Education Inc., 2011. 793. Print.

Hendrickson, Kenneth E. Jr. The Spanish-American War. Westport, CT: Greenwood Press, 2003.43-45, 55-61, 71, 74. Print.

Hernandez, Miguel J. "Kris vs. Krag." Military History (Lexington, VA) Jun 2006: 58-65. History Study Center. Web. July 19, 2019.

Hillstrom, Kevin, and Laurie Collier Hillstrom. Defining Moments: The Spanish-American War. Detroit, MI: Omnigraphics, Inc., 2012.72-98. PDF File.

The Philippine-American War, State Department: https://history.state.gov/milestones/1899-1913/war

Hispanic Division, Library of Congress. "Introduction" The World of 1898: The Spanish American War. Library of Congress, n.d. Web. July 19, 2019. http://www.loc.gov/rr/hispanic/1898/index.html

Kramer, Paul A. "United States Colonial Rule in the Philippines." Encyclopedia of Western Colonialism since 1450. Ed. Thomas Benjamin. Vol. 3. Detroit: Macmillan Reference USA, 2007. 1095-1098.

Paschall, Rod. "FOLLY IN THE Philippines!' MHQ: The Quarterly Journal of Military History Autumn 2010: 78-87,7. History Study Center. Web. July 19, 2019.

San Juan Jr., E. "U.S. Genocide in the Philippines: A Case of Guilt, Shame, or Amnesia?" Teaching American History Project: A Case of Guilt, Shame, or Amnesia? The Philippine-American War. Kevin Mariano. Eastcon, 2014. 5. PDF. http://www.eastconn.org/tah/1112KM4_ACaseGuiltShameAmnesiaPhilippineAmericanlesson.pdf

Schoonover, Thomas. Uncle Sam's War of 1898 and the Origins of Globalization. Lexington, KY: The University Press of Kentucky, 2003. 76-78, 83-85,89-101, 120-121. Print.

GMU, Manifest Destiny: McKinley defends US expansionism: http://historymatters.gmu.edu/d/5575/

Smith, lain R., and Andreas Stucki. "The Colonial Development of Concentration Camps (1868-1902)2" Journal of Imperial & Commonwealth History 39.3 (2011): 423-425. Academic Search Premier. Web. July 19, 2019.

Traxel, David. 1898. New York, NY: Alfred A. Knopf, Inc., 1998. 141,

Brown, John C. Gentleman Soldier: John Clifford Brown & the Philippine-American War, ed. Joseph McCallus. College Station: Texas A&M University Press, 2004.

Bryan, Jennings. Bryan on Imperialism: Speeches, Newspapers Articles and Interviews by Williams Jennings Bryan. Ed. Gregg, Charles, Chicago: Bently and Company, 1900.

Congressional Records. 55thCongress. 3rdSession.

Congressional Records. 56thCongress. 2ndSession. Division of Insular Affairs.

Charles, Edward. Report on the Legal Status of the Territory and Inhabitants of the Islands Acquired by the United States During the War with Spain, Considered with Reference to the Territorial Boundaries, the Constitution, and Laws of the United States. Washington, D.C.: Government Printing Office, 1900.

Davis, George. Letter to Frank Baldwin. Frank D Baldwin: Original 1902 War Letters. Swem Library Special Collections, Williamsburg, Virginia.

Elliott, Charles. The Philippines: To the End of the Commission Government: A Study in Tropical Democracy. Indianapolis: Bobbs-Merrill, 1917.

Funston, Frederick. Memories of Two Wars: Cuban and Philippine Experiences. New York: Charles Scribner's Sons,1911.

Graff, Henry ed. American Imperialism and the Philippine Insurrection: Testimony Taken from Hearings on Affairs in the Philippine Islands before the Senate Committee on the Philippines-1902. Boston: Little Brown and Company, 1969.

Los Angeles Times, January 1, 1898-Febuary, 3,1899.

Meyer, D.E. "The Massacre of Balangiga" in Balangiga: Being an Authentic Account by Several of the Few Survivors. James Taylor, ed. Joplin: McCarin Printing Company, 1931.

Military Governor of the Philippines. Annual Report of Major General Adna R. Chaffee, United States Army, Commanding the Division of the Philippines. vol. 1, Manila: The Department of the Pacific, 1902.

Military Governor of the Philippines. "General Arthur MacArthur's Philippine Campaigns: Operations 1899." RG Box 20 Papers of Gen. Arthur MacArthur 1845-1912. The MacArthur Memorial Archives and Library. Military Governor of the Philippines. John, R.M. The Philippine Insurrection against the United States: A Compilation of Documents with Notes and Introduction. Ed. Eugenio Lopez Foundation, Pasay City, P.I.: Eugenio Lopez Foundation, 1971.

United States Army. Correspondence Relating to the War with Spain Including the Insurrection in the Philippine Islands and the China Relief Expedition April 15, 1898 to July 30, 1902, Vol. 2 Washington, D.C.: United States Army, 1993.

Williams, Daniel R. The Odyssey of the Philippine Commission. Chicago: A.C. McClurg & Co., 1913.Willis, Henry. Our Philippine Problem: A Study of American Colonial Policy. New York: Henry Holt and Company, 1905.

Abinales, Patrico N. "The U.S. Army as an Occupying Force in Muslim Mindanao, 1899-1913." In Colonial Crucible: Empire in the Making of the Modern American State, ed. McCoy, Alfred and

Scarano, Francisco. 199-210. Madison: University of Wisconsin Press, 2009.

Beisner, Robert. Twelve Against Empire: The Anti-Imperialists, 1898-1900. New York: McGraw-Hill Book Company,1968.

Bolton, Grania. "Military Negotiation and National Diplomacy: Insurgent-American Relations After the Fall of Manila." Military Affairs. Vol. 36 (1972):99-104.

Castaneda, Anna Leah Fidelis T. "Spanish Structure, American Theory: The Legal Foundations of a Tropical New Deal in the Philippine Islands, 1898-1935." In Colonial Crucible: Empire in the Making of the Modern American State, ed. Alfred McCoy and Francisco Scarano, 365-375. Madison: University of Wisconsin Press, 2009.

Coffman, Edward The Regulars: The American Army, 1898-1941 Cambridge, Mass: Harvard University press, 2004.Encyclopedia Britannica Online. s.v. "audiencia." accessed February 21, 2016. http://www.britannica.com/topic/audiencia.

Garel, Grunder and Livezey, William. The Philippines and the United States. Norman: University of Oklahoma Press, 1951.

Gates, John M. "Inherent Problems in Counter-Guerilla Warfare." Major Problems in American Military History, ed. John Chambers and G. Phiehler, 240-246. New York: Houghton Mifflin Company, 1999.

Gates, John M. Schoolbooks and Krags: The United States Army in the Philippines, 1898-1902.Westport, CN: Greenwood Press, 1973.

Gates, John M. "War-Related Deaths in the Philippines, 1898-1902." Pacific Historical Review53 (1984): 367-378

Gedacht, Joshua. "Mohammedan Religion Made it Necessary to Fire: Massacres on the American Imperil Frontier from South Dakota to the Southern Philippines." In Colonial Crucible: Empire in the Making of the Modern American State, ed. McCoy, Alfred and

Scarano, Francisco. 199-210. Madison: University of Wisconsin Press, 2009.

Hutchcroft, Paul. "Colonial Masters, National Politicos, and Provincial Lords: Central Authority and Local Autonomy in the American Philippines, 1900-1913." The Journal of Asian Studies59, (2000): 277-306.

Hutchcroft, Paul "The Hazards of Jeffersonianism: Challenges of State Building in the United States and its Empire" in Colonial Crucible: Empire in the Making of the Modern American State, ed. Alfred McCoy and Francisco Scarano, 375-393. Madison: University of Wisconsin Press, 2009.

Kramer, Paul. The Blood of Government: Race, Empire, the United States & the Philippines. Chapel Hill: University of North Carolina, 2006.

Kramer, Paul. "Race, Empire, and Transnational History." In Colonial Crucible: Empire in the Making of the Modern American State, ed. McCoy, Alfred and Scarano, Francisco. 199-210. Madison: University of Wisconsin Press, 2009.

LaFever, Walter The American Age: United States Foreign Policy at Home and Abroad Since 1750. New York: Norton, 1989.

Linn, Brian. The Philippine War 1899-1902. Lawrence: University Press of Kansas, 2000.

Linn, Brian. The U.S. Army and Counterinsurgency in the Philippine War, 1899-1902. Chapel Hill: University of North Carolina Press, 1998.

Lynch, Owen J. "The U.S. Constitution and Philippine Colonialism: An Enduring and Unfortunate Legacy." in Colonial Crucible: Empire in the Making of the Modern American State, ed. Alfred McCoy and Francisco Scarano, 353-365. Madison: University of Wisconsin Press, 2009.

Mcoy, Alfred. Policing America's Empire: The United States, the Philippines, and the Rise of the Surveillance State. Madison: University of Wisconsin Press, 2006.

Miller, Stuart. Benevolent Assimilation: The American Conquest of the Philippines, 1899-1903.New Haven: Yale University Press, 1982.

Reed, John S. "External Discipline During Counterinsurgency: A Philippine War Case Study, 1900-1901." The Journal of American-East Asian Relations4 (1995): 29-48.

Reynaldo, Ieto C. "The Philippine-American War: Friendship and Forgetting" in Vestiges of War: The Philippine-American War and the Aftermath of an Imperial Dream, 1899-1999." ed. Angel Velasco Shaw, and Luis H. Francia, New York: New York University Press, 2002.

Sibley, David. A War of Frontier and Empire: the Philippine-American War, 1899-1902. New York: Hill and Wang, 2008.

Stathis, Stephen. Landmark Debates in Congress: From the Declaration of Independence to the War with Iraq. Washington: CQ Press, 2009.

Webster, Sidney "The New Philippine Government." The North American Review vol. 175, 550 (1902): 299-303.

Wolff, Leon. Little Brown Brother: How the United States Purchased and Pacified the Philippine Islands at the Century's Turn. Garden City, NY: Doubleday& Company, 1961

Brands, H.W. Bound to Empire: The United States and the Philippines. New York: Oxford University Press, 1992. Print.

Trump tells fake story about US general slaughtering 49 Muslims using bullets dipped in pig's blood, in resurfaced video https://www.independent.co.uk/news/world/americas/us-politics/trump-muslims-general-pershing-pigs-blood-video-a8829676.html